WAITING ON GOD

Spending Time in His Presence
in Silence, Stillness & Expectation

MICHAEL VAN VLYMEN

ISBN: 978-1-948680-06-6

INTRODUCTION

Why have I decided to write a book about waiting on God? The short and simple answer is that learning to wait on God was the key thing that opened up the realm of His kingdom to me. All the things that I heard the Lord was still doing, I was able to realize the truth of them by waiting on God and spending time in His presence. It seemed like I had been outside looking in forever and then suddenly found the door... found access, and my life has never been the same. Knowing about scripture suddenly became knowing it. Reading about the angels became interaction with them for the purposes of God. Desiring gifts and words of knowledge became walking in them. My walk with God was always real but this was something powerful and new. It was like I had once read the stories but now I was actually a part of the story. The lives I read about in the bible had become my life too. Is that too bold of a statement for you? I hope not. Listen to this verse...

But as it is written: "Eye has not seen, nor ear heard, Nor have entered into the heart of man The things which God has prepared for those who love Him." (1 Corinthians 2:9 NKJV)

Having discovered this treasure, I had a passion and a mandate from the Lord to share it. Just like when I learned about deliverance and how everyone could walk in freedom, I told everyone who would listen. I'm kind of in the same situation here. I absolutely know beyond any and all doubt that once you experience a visitation of the Lord your life will never be the same. I desire that for you.

Another wonderful thing about having this revelation is that it applies across the board to everything you can think of. Want to feel and experience God's presence more in your life? Wait on the Lord. Do you desire to hear His voice more clearly? Yes, wait on the Lord. How about moving more powerfully in the gifts or see the fruit of the holy Spirit more in your life? You guessed it. Waiting on God brings you to the place where the kingdom is open to you. Whether it be healings, deliverances, knowing your authority in Christ, angels and working with them, visitations of the Lord Jesus, heavenly encounters or anything else you find in the word of God, you can be sure that waiting on God will propel you into a life of biblical proportion.

But why the book? Well, those of you who know me know that the Lord taught me the things I talk about and then gave me an instruction to share those things. I have tried to do that to the best of my ability but it is really difficult to cover everything in all it's nuance in a couple of pages in a book or an hour in a teaching series. There are always questions and I decided to write something that fills in the blanks so to speak. I will take my own life as example and share with you all the little details that may mean nothing or may mean everything. The point is why leave anything out that may be a key for someone? This book will lay out as fully as possible what my life of waiting on God looks like and the fruit that it has born. I will try to address all the questions people have asked on this topic and hopefully give a full and satisfying answer for all.

The first couple of chapters I will lay a foundation through scripture about why I believe and share what I believe. I am no bible scholar nor am I a theologian so this book as my previous books will be hands on, practical, simple and understandable instruction backed up by scripture. I have no interest in writing about theory.

I pray that you will take the things presented here and prayerfully consider them and apply them to your life.

Michael

Table of Contents

PREFACE

Several years ago, I had a powerful experience with God. Actually, the encounter was with an angel of the Lord, but because the angels heed the voice of God, I know the visitation was from Him.

It was very early in the morning, as my prayer time of waiting on God normally run from about midnight to three, and I had been sitting in my prayer chair for a while just enjoying God's presence. I was at rest but focused on sensing anything that might happen no matter how small it might be. (you know sometimes the Lord speaks in a whisper) As I sat there in listening mode, something more than a whisper happened. I suddenly felt the presence of an angel enter the room from my right. I could literally feel an overwhelming presence that I might describe as a force field. It was powerful yet comfortable and I was restrained yet excited about what the Lord was about to do.

Although I could not see this angel, I could feel his presence quite well and I felt him move to a position in front of me and to my left. He stopped there. I waited to see what would happen next.

I must admit that I was excited. I like it when the Lord speaks to me in subtle ways, such as through an impression or a verse of scripture, but encounters with the Lord or His angels are pretty awesome events. I was expectant. Suddenly this angel began to speak. He said "This is the message for the servants of the Lord...." His voice was like thunder. It was beyond thunder. The words this angel spoke literally hit me like a giant sound wave that I thought would tear me apart. My whole being was shaking. My only thought at that point was to run, but I could hardly even move because of this incredible power upon me. I fell forward out of my chair onto the floor and literally crawled out of the room, and out of his presence.

Once I had processed everything later, I was really disappointed in myself for missing the visitation of the Lord because of my fear. God in His mercy came back the following night in a dreamlike experience and delivered the message for the "servants of the Lord" in a way I could receive it. It was only after I had been given the message did the Lord allow me to know it was given by the very same angel who had come the night before. The angel had veiled himself this time so that I could receive the message.

One Month Ago

My wife Gordana and I were staying with some friends for a few days enjoying some great fellowship together. This brother's prayer chair was situated in a room very close to the room we were sleeping in and I decided to take advantage of that. I knew by the spirit that something powerful was going to happen.

Here is my journal entry for that night.

September 4th 2018 approx. 12:40 am

I went to the office at about midnight and sat in the prayer chair. I sat in the chair for about twenty minutes, praying, repenting and asking the Lord for a greater sanctification and anointing for my life. Then I prayed a semblance of the Lord's prayer, using my own words but following Jesus' instruction.

After about twenty minutes, the first thing that happened was my spiritual eyes opened and I saw there were many doors in the room in the spirit. There was a door just to my right that was partially open, and I was prompted of the Lord to get up from the chair and open the door completely, which I did. I went back to the chair and at this point I was not so much

2

praying as I was waiting, watching and listening to see what would happen next.

A few minutes later, perhaps fifteen or twenty, a powerful angel came into the room and stood before me. I did not see this angel but felt his presence in a way that was both tangible and overwhelming. It felt very much like I was sitting in some kind of electrical force field. It wasn't painful, but it was powerful. This whole situation reminded me of a similar visitation I had from an angel of the Lord where I literally crawled out of the room. (which I shared above)

As the angel stood there, the Lord continued to remind me of that earlier visitation. I had a strong impression from the Lord at this point. He was telling me that I have a choice. Do I want to run away because it is uncomfortable, or stay in his presence to see what He has for me?

Knowing I had a choice, I chose to stay.

Suddenly I was covered with a powerful presence of the Lord that felt like electrical currents coursing through my body and I began to shake. This continued for several minutes.

Then my mouth began to open and close rapidly as if I was talking, without any effort or thought on my part. This also continued for several minutes. This whole experience so far was very challenging for me and was only getting more so. My feet then lifted off the floor about a foot or so, again with no intention or effort on my part.

With each new challenging event, I heard the voice of the Lord say "Do you want to run away, or will you stay?" I had an understanding, perhaps because I had been through something like this before that I could run from this experience or I could trust God.

I thought at this point that perhaps my hands would also lift into the air from their place on the arm rests of the chair, but that didn't happen. Just a few minutes later, I was launched into the stars and found myself traveling through the heavens at an incredible speed. After reaching a place very high in the heavenlies, I found myself coming back to the Earth, but this time the stars I was traveling through were displayed like a giant map. I saw writings upon this map, as if directions and strategies were notated.

I came down upon the Earth to a place where an angel was giving instruction about a particular place upon the Earth, and he was using a giant globe to illustrate his instruction. The globe was perhaps four or five feet in diameter. He mentioned certain numbers that were a reference to the location. At this point as I stood there receiving this instruction, there was an explosion nearby, but another angel absorbed the impact into his own body and no harm came to me or anyone else there.

As I stood there in this strange place wondering what would happen next, I looked up and saw that snow was beginning to fall. I stood there for a while enjoying the snowfall and wondering if the Lord was going to show me anything else, or take me back to the house. Another event happened concerning snow and after about five more minutes I found myself moving again and back in the prayer chair.

What does this mean? I believe this powerful visitation from the Lord was for the whole body of Christ. I will share what the Lord showed me about this towards the end of this book along with an encouragement the Lord gave me to share.

Chapter One

What is Waiting on God?

There seem to be just as many different ideas about waiting on God, as there are people who talk about it. I personally used to believe it was one thing and had my beliefs changed through my experience with the Lord. The first time I had heard the term was in a little community church I attended with my parents as a child. It was a phrase used during the altar call. After a few minutes of people coming forward or not, the minister would say "Let's just wait on the Lord" and we would wait. We waited usually no more than a few minutes.

Waiting on God for me today has come to mean so much more. But what it meant, this idea of waiting, wasn't so obvious while looking at it from the outside.

I recently heard a minister talk about correcting on of his congregants in respect to waiting on God. The man had told him that he was spending a season "just waiting on God" and he asked the man what exactly he was doing. "I just sit in my chair and wait" was the man's response and the minister told him how foolish and un-biblical that was. He explained to the man that he was wasting his time. He said the word waiting, actually meant "waiting like a waiter in a restaurant waits on people" It was a term saying that we should be doing things and serving the Lord and that's how we get close to Him.

It's funny how you can like and respect people yet disagree so profoundly with them. You see I really like this particular minister. He has experiences in God that make me jealous. I know from listening to him that he has times where he just enjoys the presence of God and during those times, he sometimes has visitations from the Lord. The problem was that he didn't know how to explain it to this man. I am seeing that a lot. People can walk in certain things but not necessarily explain it well to others. I will try my best to explain myself as we go.

The Words We Use

When we talk about waiting on God, what are we really saying? Are we really waiting for something? Are we waiting for an answer to a prayer? Are we waiting for God to move or give us revelation or direction or accomplish His purpose in our lives? I think we can safely say yes to all of the above. There is a place for all of that.

When I use the term waiting on God, I am referring to spending time specifically and expressly for the purpose of spending time in His presence, getting to know Him, making oneself available for anything He wants to do with us, be it give us revelation, or just be with us. I'm talking about coming aside to spend time with Him.

There are names for a pattern of this type of prayer. Some call it contemplative prayer or mystical prayer or centering prayer. Although I get it, I still like to call it "waiting on God" or "waiting on the Lord" because the other names seem to carry with them a preconceived understanding of some methodology in the way we pray or seek God. For some who teach about this there is a template that they use of so many times per day or a duration of time or a way we fix an image in our thoughts etc. I'm not saying those things are wrong per se, but I like the freedom of being spirit led in my times of waiting on God.

For as many as are led by the Spirit of God, they are the sons of God. (Romans 8:14 KJV)

6

Contemplative Prayer

This is the practice of looking at or gazing at or spending time is an awareness of God. If you look up the term in a dictionary you might see them call God "the divine" or some other generic term, but we don't let the definitions of others define what we are doing and what we really mean and who we are pursuing. For the most part, I'm sorry to say, many who use this term have an "outside looking in" understanding about it. That's why you will see so many detractors about spending time in silence before God, because they have allowed others to define what that means.

The fact that people in other religions or new age practices also "meditate", or "wait" or "pray" has no bearing upon what I do to pursue my relationship with God. Will I stop praying because those in a false religion pray? Of course not. We understand that it is completely different.

There are aspects about Christian contemplation that are accurate and useful and describe in general what I am talking about. Cultivating an awareness of God and spending time focused on that awareness is highly desirable in my opinion. We think about and focus on a thousand other things and it's OK, but concerning God it isn't? I don't think so.

Mystical Prayer

Again, if you research this term, you find a lot of generic "we don't know who the real God is" type of stuff that could cause you to throw out the baby with the bath water. The fact that so many Christians have skewed understanding about mystical prayer doesn't help much.

Much like the man who told the minister in the example earlier "I just wait" it seems just too weird to be Christian or useful. I heard about an exchange with a very famous religious figure in Christianity who when asked how they pray said "I just listen." To which the interviewer queried, "And what does God say?" The reply, "Nothing. He just listens." Not to cast dispersions upon anyone, but those types of answers don't help people to understand the true nature of mystical prayer or find a value for it. Too weird, ethereal and un-helpful. If you have ever read any of my writing, you know that if I value anything it is breaking things down, giving scriptural proofs and full explanations so that they are understandable and helpful.

In the definitions I have found about mystical prayer, very few have been accurate to my particular pursuit and have been vague at best. Things like... "knowing love" or "a place of silence" or "the love within your love" are all non-answers to me. To really find what we are talking about I think we should look at the word mystic and see where that takes us.

Mystic: 1. Someone who believes in unseen realities. 2. One who believes they can have access to hidden mysteries, transcending human knowledge. 3. One who believes they can actually know God.

These are all definitions I found for the term "mystic." I believe they are all quite telling. Look at those definitions in light of these next few scriptures.

While we look not at the things which are seen, but at the things which are not seen: for the things which are seen are temporal; but the things which are not seen are eternal. (2 Corinthians 4:18 KJV)

Now faith is the substance of things hoped for, the evidence of things not seen (Hebrews 11:1 KJV)

And He said to them, "To you it has been given to know the [a]mystery of the kingdom of God; but to those who are outside, all things come in parables. (Mark 4:11 NKJV)

Jesus answered them, "To you it has been granted to know the mysteries of the kingdom of heaven, but to them it has not been granted. (Matthew 13:11 NASB)

"This is eternal life, that they may know You, the only true God, and Jesus Christ whom You have sent. (John 17:3 NASB)

We are from God; he who knows God listens to us; he who is not from God does not listen to us. By this we know the spirit of truth and the spirit of error. (1 John 4:6 NASB)

Mystical prayer to me is prayer where I am really speaking with God, hearing His voice, connecting with Him and receiving revelation by which I can live and fulfill my destiny in God. So, in essence, all believers should be mystical as opposed to being religious.

*Just to be fair, sometimes people describe things in a way that have meaning and relevance to them that do not have the same meaning and relevance to others. I don't want to judge anyone by the terms they use to talk about their prayer life, but would rather look at the fruit their lives bear. Sometimes people describe or explain things in the most unusual ways and sincerely don't understand why people don't "get it."

Look to the Word

Looking back at the story of the pastor who told the man that waiting o the Lord was like being a waiter, is this true? Does one of the meanings of the word "wait" used in the bible in the context we are talking about, convey that meaning?

The word wait in Hebrew...

The word most often translated as wait, as in "waiting on the Lord" is the word *Qavah*.

Qavah means (1) "to bind together" (like by twisting strands together in making a rope), (2) "to look patiently," (3) "to tarry or wait," and (4) "to expect, hope or look eagerly with expectation."

This word is used in places like Psalm 25:5

> *Lead me in thy truth, and teach me: for thou art the God of my salvation;* **on thee do I wait all the day.** *(Psalm 25:5 KJV)*

> **I wait for the LORD, my soul does wait**, *And in His word do I hope. My soul waits for the Lord More than the watchmen for the morning; Indeed, more than the watchmen for the morning. (Psalm 130:5-6 NASB)*

Some have said that the meaning of this word was translated incorrectly by bible scholars. In these verses that were translated as "wait", those who believe it means being like a waiter, are looking at the meaning of qavah strictly as "to bind together," reasoning that if we are doing things for the Lord, such as studying the scriptures and doing His will, it is like twisting strands together to make a strong rope that binds our lives to Him.

I believe that the translators who worked on this translated it correctly. If you look at Psalm 130, you see that this verse denotes the passage of time, and along with that, an expectation. Like watchmen who watch through the night as they guard the city walls look with expectation for the morning, David waits for the Lord. To me, this verse shows very clear the meaning of waiting and looking with an expectation.

Therefor, when I talk about waiting on God or waiting on the Lord, and I use Psalm 25:5 as a scriptural permission if you will, you know why.

Believing God to Visit Us

The understanding of the pastor who thought it was foolish to "just wait" is pretty much the prevailing thought on the subject, even by those really seeking a visitation from God. The whole concept doesn't make sense to our natural minds. Let me get this straight... I do absolutely nothing and God visits me in the most supernatural, awesome and biblical way? Yes, pretty much. (although there is some understanding we need to have) But if I do stuff to cause God to visit me, it doesn't happen? Yes. That can be true too.

I have had stern rebukes from people in ministry about sharing these things. "You're giving people false hope Mike. Yes, God did this for me, but only because I have been a faithful servant of the Lord for thirty-five years." "This is not for everyone" I have heard said many, many times. Many have a hard time coming to grips with the fact that God will visit the one who just got born again, when there are people that have been working in the church for years that haven't even had a visitation of the Lord. (at least not that they were able to perceive)

I liken this process to a romantic relationship between a man and woman in a marriage. Although there are proofs we have in our actions that show our love and intention, we are not earning love or the show of love. The out-workings of our love is a given. We are setting aside time to be intimate with the one we love. "Just sit with me a while." Have you ever done that? Have you ever spent time with the one you love and not uttered a word? Have you spent time in the same room just because you want to be near them?

We are cultivating intimacy with the Lord.

One of the saying we have in our family is "come over so I can look at you." Do you know what that means? When my son Matt comes over to visit and he tells me "Dad, I've got a couple hours free. How about I cut the grass for you?" My response is always something like "how about we sit down and spend some time together? Let's talk. Let's visit. Time is too precious, I can cut the grass later." Yes, just let me look at you. You don't have to do anything for me, and as a matter of fact I would rather have your fellowship than your work. Does that make sense? If you feel that way, how do you think the Lord feels?

Waiting on the Lord is setting aside our time and our agenda to make ourselves available to Him. Waiting on the Lord is telling the Lord "Lord, I will wait for you, just in case you show up. Just the idea that there is a chance to be with you is worth it to me."

Again, going back to the idea of relationship... When you fell in love did you ever go somewhere even *hoping* to see the one that made your heart jump? Waiting on the Lord is the expectation of seeing Him, being with Him and spending time in His presence. The expectation of smelling the fragrance of the Lord and the hope that comes from what His presence brings.

What does the bible say about love? What does true love look like. We remember Mary and Martha from the gospel of Luke. Obviously they both loved Jesus but Martha felt that the commitment of service should come first and Mary "selfishly" wanted to sit at Jesus' feet.

> *38 Now it came to pass, as they went, that he entered into a certain village: and a certain woman named Martha received him into her house.*
>
> *39 And she had a sister called Mary, which also sat at Jesus' feet, and heard his word.*
>
> *40 But Martha was cumbered about much serving, and came to him, and said, Lord, dost thou not care that my*

sister hath left me to serve alone? bid her therefore that she help me.

41 And Jesus answered and said unto her, Martha, Martha, thou art careful and troubled about many things:

42 But one thing is needful: and Mary hath chosen that good part, which shall not be taken away from her. (Luke 10:38-42 KJV)

Jesus told Martha that Mary had chosen the good part. Here is Jesus' answer in the Passion Translation.

41 The Lord answered her, "Martha, my beloved Martha. Why are you upset and troubled, pulled away by all these many distractions? Are they really that important? 42 Mary has discovered the one thing most important by choosing to sit at my feet. She is undistracted, and I won't take this privilege from her." (Luke 10:41-42 TPT)

Jesus said that the important thing was to sit at His feet. Intimacy and not service or works was the preferred thing.

Our Comfort Level

Many times, it might indeed be easier or more comfortable to keep ourselves busy before for the Lord as opposed to being still and quiet before Him. That time of silence is one where the Holy Spirit will often talk to us about the issues of our hearts. The Lord desires to bring revelation to us but also a purging of all that doesn't belong. The time of waiting on the Lord is a time where God can do a deep work within us.

We wait for him. We are quiet and still before Him. He shows up and He does the work. It's all Him. He gets all the glory. We have done nothing to receive this goodness from Him except make ourselves available to receive from Him. We wait for Him with an expectation.

13

Waiting with expectation

I have used this example many times but I feel it illustrated perfectly that we can wait for the Lord with expectation.

Let's fantasize for a moment that Bill Gates or some other very wealthy and powerful person has taken a liking to you for whatever reason. They told you...

"I like you. I want to help you, I want to do something substantial for you. I want to meet you to make this happen. I am going to be coming through your town this week. I am not sure which day, but would you be willing to go to the train station every day this week and wait for me for a couple of hours at this certain time? Will you do that?"

Talk about waiting with expectation! I am quite sure that you would not only be honored and overjoyed at your good fortune, but you would be fantasizing about what exactly this visitation could mean for you and your life and future. You would be making plans, You would be dreaming about how this could change everything! "Is today the day?" you would be asking yourself. Wow! He wants to meet with me to do something for me.

Maybe he'll pay off all my debts. Maybe I'll get to finish school. I might be set up in business. Maybe he will allow me to use his name as a reference to open doors. Yes, we would all be waiting with excitement and expectation.

The God of all creation wants to be that person in our lives.

Being Transparent

Waiting on the Lord to me is like coming into a knowing that all of your dreams are about to come true. It's about coming into such a profound state of rest that you just yield to His presence and power and love overtaking you. It is putting yourself into a position whereby you can step into the spiritual dimension, knowing that the word says that we should walk in the spirit by laying aside everything our flesh and soul says is important. Make no mistake, your flesh will fight you on this.

When the day is done and I have dealt with all the things we must deal with in normal everyday life, I see the clock is getting close to midnight and anticipation begins to build in me. Waiting on the Lord is the place where my spirit soars and my soul is overwhelmed and my flesh is cleansed and placed in its proper place of submission to my spirit.

Waiting on the Lord is coming into the secret place in God, just He and I in fellowship together. It is the place where the veil is removed and heavenly realities are manifest right before me. In this place of intimacy with God the things of heaven are accessible. The sights and sounds, worship, angels, fragrances and other manifestations of His presence overwhelm your senses as the natural realm pales in comparison to the heavenly realm.

There is an alignment that takes place in this place of waiting. It is an alignment of our life, our priorities, values where true levels of importance are discerned. The things of the world, of the flesh begin to have their proper perspective in our lives. The disappointments, fear, concerns, desires, goals, hopes and dreams all come into their correct place of importance or unimportance.

I heard a testimony once from someone who was taken up before the throne of God and the Lord told this person to take everything out of their pockets and place it on the altar. All of the treasures and things they held so dear of this world, suddenly, before the throne of God, had their true value revealed. They said it was as if they had taken trash out of their pockets and laid it on the altar. All the goals of this life, the cars, houses, careers and normal human plans could not compare to the glory of God. That's why we must hold the things of this world loosely.

Please don't misread what I'm telling you. I'm not saying you shouldn't have goals or cars or houses but rather that you should have a kingdom perspective of all these things,

But seek first the kingdom of God and His righteousness, and all these things shall be added to you. (Matthew 6:33 NKJV)

The Throne of Grace

When you are waiting on God you are not just waiting. You are coming before the throne of grace by faith. You are coming into the presence of God. The veil is torn and you have access. Knowing that the veil was set in place by God to separate a place for the most holy from the holy. In other words, the ark was placed in a place that was not accessible to everyone and the veil was the barrier and the door. When the veil was torn, the door was thrown wide open and we have access into the very presence of God.

It is important that we think of these things as realities and know that they are realities and not dismiss these things as so often we may have done in the past. Our hope is in Him. Realizing that every answer we seek, every problem we face and every desire of our heart can be satisfied in Him.

When I wait on the Lord this awareness overtakes me because I have set aside the natural, the carnal and the presence of God is manifestly discernable in these times. My hope is restored and my fears are vanquished before Him.

Chapter Two

What Prompts Someone to Wait on God?

There is a holy discontent that I believe is God given to drive us closer into the Lord's arms. There is a knowing that we could be closer to Him, to know Him more and better. It is an awareness of that God sized hole that only He can fill that causes us to pursue Him so that we might experience that satisfaction. We get this. We understand this, but what is it that causes us to "wait" on God?

Most of the writing I have seen about waiting on God, even in the case of David, has been from the aspect of waiting for answers to prayers. In general, that seems to be the common understanding. We pray and then we wait on God for the answer. Although that is true also, you understand that is not what we are talking about here. We are waiting for the Lord Himself and not for those things we have asked of Him. Again, using the example of loving relationship...

I like it when Gordana comes home from work. Sometimes when I know she is on the way I will sit outside and wait for her. What is my excitement or anticipation about? Am I excited to see her because I am hoping she will prepare supper? Maybe she will do the laundry and my favorite T-shirt will be back on the shelf. Maybe I'm waiting for her so that she will straighten my office. No, I don't wait for any of those reasons. Likewise, I'm not waiting so that I can do things for her. Although I do enjoy doing things that make her happy, there is something more bonding about spending quiet time together as opposed to doing things.

The reason I wait for her is because I love her. I enjoy being with her. I like to see her smile. I want to hear her voice and have fellowship with her. You see, all the reasons I fell in love with her in the first place are the same reasons why I wait for her. I have joy in her presence.

The bible says...

Thou wilt shew me the path of life: in thy presence is fulness of joy; at thy right hand there are pleasures for evermore. (Psalm 16:11 KJV)

Although David did have to wait for certain things to come to pass in his life, such as waiting twenty years to become king, but the scripture above is talking about being in His presence.

1 To You, O Lord, I lift up my soul. 2 O my God, in You I trust, Do not let me be ashamed; Do not let my enemies exult over me. 3 Indeed, none of those who wait for You will be ashamed; Those who deal treacherously without cause will be ashamed. 4 Make me know Your ways, O Lord; Teach me Your paths. 5 Lead me in Your truth and teach me, For You are the God of my salvation; **For You I wait all the day**. (Psalm 25:1-5 NASB)

David's desire in waiting for the Lord is quite obvious in the scriptures.

As the deer pants for water, so I long for you, O God. 2 I thirst for God, the living God...(Psalm 42:1-2 TLB)

What Stirs up Such Passion for God?

Many years ago, when I was in my mid-twenties, the Lord delivered me from satan's grasp and it was the turning point of my life. I was beyond grateful to Him. I had grown up in a church culture that definitely did not teach nor display the power of God, so when He revealed Himself to me as a powerful deliverer, it changed everything. I went from knowing about a God, to being in love with God. I knew Him as my deliverer. I still did not know a lot at that time, but I knew about praying and talking to Him and singing to Him (worship) so that is what I did.

I loved to say the name "Jesus." I loved the way it sounded. I loved the way it felt to say it and the way I felt when I said it. It felt like hope and power coming out of my mouth. I loved to sing about His power and love and how He could change lives, because He had changed mine. I would sing songs that lifted up His name and sing His name really loudly. My favorite times singing to Him or worshipping Him were when I was driving along in my car. I was alone with Him. No one else around, just He and I, and it was an intimate experience for me. I would talk to Him and sing and worship for hours if I had the opportunity to do so.

Every time I saw someone get set free or I saw the power of God on display, it only caused me to love Him more. It wasn't exactly waiting on God as I know it now, but it was me drawing closer to Him and Him drawing closer to me.

7 Submit therefore to God. Resist the devil and he will flee from you. 8 **Draw near to God and He will draw near to you**. Cleanse your hands, you sinners; and purify your hearts, you double-minded. (James 4:7-8 NASB)

At that time, it wasn't so much that I was asking for things from Him, I was just watching to see what He would do next. I was in awe of Him. I think David was also in awe of Him. If you read through the Psalms you see it plainly.

Joining the Ranks of Enoch and Company

It was about ten years ago that I began to hear stories of people being visited by the Lord, miracles of biblical proportion, visitations by angels and other such phenomenon. I wasn't exactly sure how I felt about it all at the time, but I had by that time seen some supernatural things and I was kind of hopeful. It didn't hurt that the girl who first told us about all these things was herself a walking advertisement for God's presence. She would get covered in gold sparkles when she talked about the Lord.

My wife had a friend who was sharing all of these incredible stories with us and we believed. We soon learned that there were quite a few people who knew about, and or walked in these things and as we heard more accounts of people living this supernatural lifestyle, our hunger to walk in these things also grew. Our quest to walk in the deep things of God was born and we relentlessly pursued that desire for several years.

Our problem at this time was that although we found people who walked in these things and were willing to talk about it, we didn't find anyone giving out instruction of how we could also walk in these things. (at least not in a plain enough way that we could follow it)

So, this is what we had.... People would tell these accounts of having visitations from the Lord and His angels, meeting people from the cloud of witnesses like Enoch and Elijah, going into the realms of Heaven and seeing the wonders there, seeing into the unseen realm as readily as they saw in the seen realm, but then not sharing in a practical way how we could also have this life. It was frustrating. We went to conference after conference, meeting after meeting and event after event hoping to find someone who could help us get that breakthrough into this incredible life.

After several years of searching, (it wasn't fruitless searching because we were learning things) we finally heard an instruction about how to wait on God for breakthrough into the heavenly realm. I heard the instruction on June tenth, 2010 and got the first real breakthrough two days later. Does that tell you why I am so excited to talk about waiting on God? But wait! Is this about pursuing God or manifestations of the spiritual realm?

You learn very quickly that everything flows out of relationship with Jesus Christ. All the things of Heaven flow from and through Him. But you also come to understand as you hear the testimonies of those who walk in these things that this is not some kind of strange addition to your Christian walk, but is in fact the full, or fuller manifestation of being who you are created to be. After one or two experiences with God you understand that yes, we are meant to walk with God like Enoch. We are also meant to have encounters with Heaven like Ezekiel, and we are meant to have revelation like John. We came to understand that although we are in fact pursuing a closer and deeper walk with the Lord, as we fulfilled that desire, the things of Heaven, the revelation of God, and the angelic realm also manifested around us. It was very much like you couldn't have one without the other.

How is it then that there are devoted servants of God who spend their whole lives studying the word of God, spending time in prayer and the preaching of the word, don't have these manifestations of the Kingdom of God in their lives? I knew the answer from looking back at my own life. There is a verse in scripture that sums it up nicely.

27 And when Jesus departed thence, two blind men followed him, crying, and saying, Thou son of David, have mercy on us.

28 And when he was come into the house, the blind men came to him: and Jesus saith unto them, **Believe ye that I am able to do this? They said unto him, Yea, Lord**.

Then touched he their eyes, saying, **According to your faith be it unto you**. (Matthew 9:27-29 KJV)

According to our Faith we Receive

Like me, most believers were studying the life of Daniel, Ezekiel or Enoch, but not saying "Lord I want to have a life like Daniel, Ezekiel or Enoch." We grew up knowing that they were special people and that just wasn't going to happen.

According to our faith we receive. This is how we can have so many books or sermons about angels from those who have never even met one (as far as they know) or about miracles, who write very authoritatively from a historical context and understanding. To experience the things of the kingdom it seems that we must believe. The belief part comes first.

Jesus *said to her, "Did I not say to you that if you believe, you will see the glory of God?" (John 11:40 NASB)

The thing about believing that you can't have a life like those in the bible, is that it causes you to reject that as reality and disdain those who do believe it. Even for those people kind enough not to mock believing believers, they still think they are "off" at best. God doesn't seem to force this life upon people. For those who teach from the pulpit with authority that God doesn't do the miraculous anymore, they are stealing from people the rich life in God that they are meant to live. I can't believe that the Lord is very happy about this.

But woe unto you, scribes and Pharisees, hypocrites! for ye shut up the kingdom of heaven against men: for ye neither go in yourselves, neither suffer ye them that are entering to go in. (Matthew 23:13 KJV)

There Comes a Point

I was speaking with a friend not long ago about his desire to see the unseen and have experiences in God like those talked about in the bible. He told me he has been seeking for many years the kind of breakthrough I talk about. He has spent time in prayer, he has taken all the steps. What is next? My helpful advice to him? Get extreme. What? He has been actively pursuing this life. What do you mean "get extreme?"

I was very open with him about this. I told him what extreme looks like. There is a reason that most will not do the kinds of things I talk about. It doesn't seem normal. It is during this time of contemplation that people reach a point. The point is the place where we have a couple of different voices speaking to us. One voice says, "It shouldn't be this hard." "If it is God, it shouldn't take such effort from us."

It is during this time that you remember all of the supernatural people that have told you that it will just come when it is time. All of the famous teachers and preachers that say it's so easy to see and interact with Heaven and the Lord and the angels, come to mind at this juncture. Then there is another voice that says, "Go for it!" "You want this so do everything you can to lay hold of it."

About 10 years ago I was determined to get into shape after several years of neglecting my health. I finally got to the point where I said "I'm going to do this even if it kills me." The reality was that it did challenge me. It was hard to do. Simple but hard. The amazing thing was though that I did not die. I got into shape. There came a point where I made the decision that would position me for the breakthrough.

I told my friend what I do for breakthrough. He told me not long after "Mike I'm doing it. I want this so I'm doing it." He came to that point of decision. His desire to participate in the things of Heaven exceeded his desire for comfort. What was happening in his life that was prompting him to desire to wait on God? I believe in his case it was a combination of his heritage and his community. He is surrounded by people who walk in the supernatural of God, and that is his heritage as well.

Community is a great thing for providing the atmosphere for breakthrough. Placing yourself in the right atmosphere, hearing the testimonies, being in that spiritual dynamic will give you desire.

Are Steps of Faith Always Really Easy?

The truth is that the Lord does make it simple so that all can understand and enter in who desire to do so. The major blockage many face is the desire that God do something sovereign so they don't have to do something they don't quite have understanding for. Many times, God asks us to take the step of faith before He give us the understanding of that step. Much like it talks about in the account of when Jesus raised up Lazarus...

Jesus said to her, "Did I not say to you that if you would believe you would see the glory of God?" (John 11:40 NKJV)

Jesus is making a statement to Martha here that we can take something away from. Believe in Him and all things are possible. This really is a life of trusting God.

Several years ago, the Lord began to make it very plain to us that He was our provider. A time we really needed to see His hand at work was when we needed to put the kids in a different school and we needed to move to do that. I felt the Lord was telling us to move, to go, but I had no idea where that would be or how we could make it happen.

By faith Abraham obeyed when he was called to go out to the place which he would receive as an inheritance. And he went out, not knowing where he was going. (Hebrews 11:8 NKJV)

Like Abraham, I didn't know exactly what God had in mind, but I trusted. I felt the Lord was telling me to make a list of what our new home would be like, and then go to it. I knew this list was for the whole family so I told them to write down all the things they would like to have in our new house. The list they came up with was quite impressive and to be honest my faith was not quite at the same level then. But by faith we made the list of about twenty things and then began to look for our house.

For two years I put that search criteria in my computer and looked for that house. I looked in all of the reasonable areas where we might have some chance of finding that miracle. Some might say that the two-year search was in essence waiting on God of a sort, but the truth was that He answered that prayer the very week we made our list and prayed. You see, when I finally searched in the most affluent neighborhood, I found the house and every item on the list was present. I read the description online and I thought there must be some kind of typo because there was no way that house was selling for that low price. The thing was that the house had been for sale for two years but was never listed until the morning I searched in that area. We drew up a purchase agreement a couple hours later and after that more than twenty people called about that house that day. The answer was found in Him. I didn't have to figure anything out.

If you will believe Him, He will give you the desires of your heart. He will provide.

So, as we wait on the Lord, we have to believe that He loves us and has great plans for us. He will provide. He will increase us. Truly as we draw close to Him, He will draw close to us!

"Draw near to God and He will draw near to you...." (James 4:8 NKJV)

Take steps of faith by waiting on the Lord and believe with a heart of expectation. He will not disappoint you.

Desire, Dissatisfaction or Both?

For me it didn't start out as dissatisfaction but something far more driving. I was fighting for my life and Jesus was the only possible answer. He showed Himself to me through the brother who ministered deliverance to me and I was overcome with desire for Him. I wanted my life to be what He wanted my life to be. If I wasn't singing to Him, I was talking to Him and if I wasn't doing either I was thinking about Him. It didn't matter the day or hour or what was going on around me my heart was fixed on Him.

I was connected to Him. There is something about knowing who you are and who loves you and watches over you. It wasn't that I had a mental understanding I had a knowing. I was a part and that drew me.

Having experienced the supernatural power of God I knew it was real beyond real. I didn't want to live a "normal" life and then cry out to the Lord only when things got bad. I wanted to live in the middle of Him. Forget about visitations, I wanted a habitation of God. My desire was to walk in that which we were created to walk in for the glory of the Lord and to see His kingdom manifested upon the Earth.

The Never-Ending Cycle

What not only prompted me to wait on the Lord but to be excited to wait on the Lord was the manifestation of His presence in these times. Many say don't look for or seek for experiences but I say although that is true, we must have balance in all things and live according to the word. I was waiting on the Lord in prayer two nights ago and after about forty-five minutes or so a powerful angel appeared and was standing a couple of feet in front of me. I didn't ask for that to happen, but God did it. So, what do I do? Do I tell the God of all creation that I don't receive what He is doing because it challenges my theology or understanding? No, I just go with it to wherever the Lord takes it. Lord Jesus you are the boss.

Here is the thing though... you have an encounter with the Lord's angel and it fills you with faith and anticipation for what God is doing in your life and it causes you to go back to waiting on the Lord the next night and the next and so on. Each new revelation just makes you more in love with Him and it drives you to the word and He gives you revelation, and then it drives you to prayer and you feel His presence and it drives you to worship and you never want it to end because you are literally in the presence of God.

There's always someone who will say "God never drives us to do anything." Perhaps that is true but the leading and the wooing of the Lord is so overwhelming that this world and the things of the world cannot compare or compete.

I am compelled and captivated by Him to the point that it makes me hunger for more of His presence. I wait on the Lord because of that, I worship the Lord because of that and I intercede before the Lord for that reason also. The bible mentions this ever-increasing flow.

But we all, with open face beholding as in a glass the glory of the Lord, are changed into the same image from glory to glory, even as by the Spirit of the Lord. (2Corinthians 3:18 KJV)

Chapter Three

My Journey

This waiting on God has been a journey of discovery for me. Listening, learning and believing that He will make things clear and grant me the desires of my heart because I know that He is a good God. Believing for Him to take me deeper to places I don't even know how to ask for...

I will instruct thee and teach thee in the way which thou shalt go: I will guide thee with mine eye. (Psalm 32:8 KJV)

When you first hear about "waiting on God" or "waiting on the Lord" you have a decision to make. Either this is true and something from the Lord or it is not and it could possibly be the enemy or a colossal waste of time. The thing is though that if you decide to pursue waiting on God you are starting out completely by faith, usually (like myself) having little to go on except testimonies that make you want to believe it's true.

The Ways we Wait

In the opening chapter I spoke of how we wait in stillness and the biblical explanation of it, but there are also other ways we wait. Yes, we wait in stillness and we wait in silence, we wait in prayer and in adoration. We wait on the Lord in worship and we wait in intercession. We also wait on the Lord simply to bask in His presence and glory to enjoy Him.

We also wait on the Lord for answers to prayer and for His timing to bring the manifestation of His will for our lives. All these are valid.

For our purposes, we are talking about the waiting on the Lord that brings breakthrough into the things of the spirit, therefor we will focus mainly on stillness, then we will talk about waiting in prayer and waiting in worship.

Waiting on God – the Basic Instruction

Many have heard me give testimony about learning to wait on God and how that was the introduction of something beyond anything I had ever experienced. The power and presence of God.

The instruction I first heard that gave me breakthrough in to the things of the spirit in my life were from my friend Bruce Allen and it was this....

"Sit still and at rest in a chair, close your eyes and look with your eyes closed, believing and expecting for God to show you something."

That was the initial instruction I received and followed. It was the "jumping off point" for me and God honored my steps of faith by showing up. The Lord met me the very first time I followed that instruction and gave me a lesson in His faithfulness to keep us safe as we pursue Him. I'm going to share it in its completeness even though I have shared in in another book, because the topic calls for a clear record of how waiting on the Lord unfolded for me and brought incredible breakthroughs in many areas of my life as well as my family.

The Morning of Breakthrough

On the twelfth of June, 2010 at approximately seven-thirty am, I went downstairs to the living room to wait on the Lord and pray according to the instruction I had received. I had the house to myself so I knew I would not be disturbed and I was excited to "try" what I had heard about waiting on the Lord. I really didn't know how to begin but to sit down in a chair and begin.

I sat down and closed my eyes. I told the Lord, "I hope this is what I've been looking for." I settled into the chair and began to focus on the Lord and spiritual truths that I knew such as the fact that He never changes, angels have been given charge over us and He is no respecter of persons. The way I experienced the time that passed was interesting in that it felt very much like a waste of time even though I was hoping against hope that something would happen of a breakthrough. As I sat there quite still in the chair with my eyes closed, I "looked" to see if I could see anything. Five minutes had gone by and I had seen nothing and sensed nothing. Ten minutes went by... nothing. Twenty minutes... nothing. At thirty minutes I felt like I was wasting my time and I felt that I should be doing something to see a breakthrough. The thing was that I had been looking for some kind of instruction for several years and this was the first and only instruction I had ever received. I continued on to give an honest attempt to what I was doing.

At forty minutes I began to think perhaps I was doing it wrong, but continued on. I was thinking purely of the function I was performing instead of realizing that God was involved and would honor my stepping out in faith.

At forty-five minutes I had the sense that a powerful presence of electricity was covering my entire body. (This is something I have neglected to tell in the past but was reminded by looking again at my journal) The electricity came first and then I began moving very fast, seemingly on a vehicle of some kind, with someone standing in front of me. I had the idea that it was probably an angel but wasn't quite sure. I was moving so fast it seemed as if I was flying. I realized at that moment that I was sitting very still in my chair and yet a part of me was moving at extreme speed at the same time. Experiencing the natural and the spiritual realms at the same time scared me and I quickly opened my eyes and jumped up from the chair.

According to my journal about an hour had past at this point. I walked around the house until I had calmed down a bit and realized that this was something I had been seeking from the

Lord for several years and I should try to trust Him more than I was. I repented for my fear and went back to the chair. I began to wait on the Lord in the same way. This time after about twenty minutes the air around me seemed to electrify and I began to hear all kinds of different sounds. The sounds got louder and louder and because I was not used to this, I questioned the source and was again afraid and jumped up from the chair. Almost immediately I was heartsick at not having trust enough in the Lord to receive this new blessing of experiencing the heavenly realm. I thought that I better get it together because I don't want to lose what God is doing. I had waited so long it seemed.

I repented, went back to the chair and began to wait on the Lord again. This time I felt absolutely no connection whatsoever. I waited and waited but to no avail. After a while I got discouraged and went back upstairs and laid on the bed. I was quite disappointed with myself and as I laid back, I talked to the Lord, "Lord I'm sorry for my fear. Please help me."

The next thing I knew, I was moving through the stars and galaxies and huge clouds made of stars and I absolutely knew the Lord was leading me as I went. I had absolutely no fear at all. I finally found myself standing in the heavens up in the stars and looking on creation. The Lord was with me there. Then just as quickly I found myself moving back to the Earth and entering the ocean and moving to the bottom of the ocean. I saw many different kinds of fish and other ocean life. I was in awe of what I was experiencing and was looking upon the sights with a sense of wonder as I stood there at the bottom.

As I stood there, I clearly heard the Lord's voice. "See? I'm with you even to the depths of the ocean."

The Lord in His mercy had taken me into Psalm 139.

If I ascend into heaven, You are there; If I make my bed in [a]hell, behold, You are there. (Psalm 139:8 NKJV)

To deal with my fear of experiencing the very thing I was asking for, the Lord gave me a powerful confirmation that He is ever present and there is no need to fear. Indeed, He never leaves us nor forsakes us. I believe the Lord Himself led me into the spiritual realm to spark confidence in me for the journey ahead.

This is a word to the body of Christ in general I believe. As we seek Him and His kingdom for His purposes, we need not fear but can move ahead boldly knowing that He is with us.

Preparing for the Journey

I spent the rest of the day electrified. I was so excited I didn't know what to do with myself. It is easy to tell those who have not quite made the transition from the natural to the spiritual realm because many ask "how real does it get? Does it seem almost as real as the natural?" The truth is that there is no comparison. Once you experience that realm, this natural realm holds little fascination for you. The spiritual realm completely overwhelms the natural realm. It is something most people have to adjust to.

Suddenly I had decisions to make. What do I do next? I had difficulty the first go-round, does this get easier or will it even happen again? It had seemed like I didn't even know what I was doing so will I gain understanding as I go? A Thousand questions rose up before me but in the end, the only thing I could do was keep it simple and try to repeat what I had done the first time and see what would happen.

I decided I would set aside time every day to wait on the Lord so that I could have this incredible fellowship with Him.

Note* As I share my journey please realize that there are keys I am sharing as testimony. There is a saying that if you want to be successful in something... "Find someone who has achieved what you are interested in, find out the price they paid to get there, and then pay that price."

I still find that valid today and I still do that.

I really had no clue on the impact this would have upon my life but I knew the goodness of God and I knew He was with me.

Every Day

As I said, I decided to wait on the Lord every day because I wanted to have a repeat of what I had experienced but also because I knew there would be more. I knew this was just the tip of the iceberg and couldn't wait to see what would come next. Initially, I decided to carve out an hour every evening where I would go to the living room and wait on God in my chair. This particular time period was hit and miss for me because although usually no one hardly used the living room and no one particularly needed me during the evening, once I started to use that hour to pray, everyone needed me at least for a moment.

I chose an hour because of the initial amount of time it took to move from the natural to the spiritual realm.

I'm very mindful of the fact that right now as people are reading this, some are saying "why do we even need that? Isn't Jesus enough?" The truth is that everything is found in Jesus so yes, He is. But the reality is that there were those who followed Him from a distance and others who were at His side. There was John who knew the very heartbeat of Jesus as he laid his head upon Jesus' chest. There were those who wanted to come and hear Jesus speak and then get a free meal afterwards and we still have that option today. I want to be like John or Elijah or Enoch or Philip who were right in the thick of it and not shying away from God's presence and power. Do you want to live a "normal" life and still attend church on Sunday? You can have that if you like. I am not interested. Waiting on the Lord has ruined me for anything but Him and His presence and power and Kingdom. Now that I know just how real it all is, I cannot live any other way. I pray that you will be the same.

1 Therefore, leaving the discussion of the elementary principles of Christ, let us go on to perfection, not laying again the foundation of repentance from dead works and of faith toward God, 2 of the doctrine of baptisms, of laying on of hands, of resurrection of the dead, and of eternal judgment. 3 And this we will do if God permits.

4 For it is impossible for those who were once enlightened, and have tasted the heavenly gift, and have become partakers of the Holy Spirit, 5 and have tasted the good word of God and the powers of the age to come, 6 if they fall away, to renew them again to repentance, since they crucify again for themselves the Son of God, and put Him to an open shame. (Hebrews 6:1-6 NKJV)

Once you have tasted, you don't want to turn away or fall away.

It seemed that praying in the evening wasn't working out so well. I would tell the kids not to interrupt me for an hour and sometimes they did ok and other times they would just have to talk to me anyway. Whispering to me while my eyes were closed... "Hey dad, can I get some money out of your desk?" The kids being kids thinking that if they whispered it wouldn't bother me so much.

I remember many times in the evening I would just get to the point where I would feel that electricity in the air and someone would shake me or speak to me and pull me away from the spiritual realm. In reality that was pretty much the norm. If you ever want to interact with someone, just start doing something else you enjoy and they will be with you shortly. In the end I came to see that it wasn't really fair to them either. Something to remember however is that any kind of being drawn to or engaged with anything physical, be it movement, sounds, smells or sights etc., can very easily pull you back from engagement with the spirit. The notable exception is that when you are *fully immersed* in the spirit, it seems almost impossible to draw you back out. An example of this might be found in Acts ten when Peter fell into a trance.

9 The next day, as they went on their journey and drew near the city, Peter went up on the housetop to pray, about [e]the sixth hour. 10 Then he became very hungry and wanted to eat; but while they made ready, he fell into a trance 11 and saw heaven opened and an object like a great sheet bound at the four corners, descending to him and let down to the earth. (Acts 10:9-11 NKJV)

Another more recent example would be Maria Woodworth-Etter who would freeze in a trance under the unction of the Holy Spirit.

On January 23, 1885 the Ft. Wayne, Indiana Gazette wrote,

"Sister Etter had been told that it was too late for Hartford City and her ministry would never find roots in this city of sin. Newspaper reporters tell of Sister Etter standing on a stump near a cornfield, for the crowd had out- grown the small building, with one hand holding her Bible and the other lifted towards heaven. Suddenly she froze before the mocking throng. Hours passed into another day and she continued to stand silent and still before the ever-growing crowds of mockers. When the crowd had grown to over 2,000 Sister Etter suddenly awoke and began to preach under a great anointing of the Holy Spirit.

The Watch of the Night

After probably a couple of months I decided to move my prayer/waiting time to a time when everyone was asleep in bed. I had to have uninterrupted time and that was my best shot. Although everyone would go to bed by eleven, a few days of trial and error showed me that as long as someone was still awake, they might come to give me last minute reminders or questions for the next day. Therefor, midnight became my starting point and by this time I had decided to increase my prayer time so I dedicated midnight until three am for prayer.

I found out later that this is called the "*third watch of the night*" and is a time of accelerated activity in the realm of the spirit. Many intercessors choose the watch of the night to pray and intercede.

This new watch of the night found me at one of several prayer places in the house. Many times, I sat in my "prayer chair", but other times I would lay on the floor close to the chair or my bed, or sometimes I would lay in bed to pray and wait, and as well I would pray in my closet sometimes. All of this was me trying to get a handle on what was the best place and position for prayer and waiting on the lord.

Looking back at all the little adjustments I was making to my efforts to wait on the Lord, it would be really easy to believe that it shouldn't be that hard or that difficult. If God really wanted you to see the things of Heaven or if He really wanted to tell you something you wouldn't have to "try." This is something your flesh normally wants to agree with. I came up with a protocol for waiting on the Lord based on scripture. I decided I would start my time of waiting on the Lord with worship and praise.

Enter into His gates with thanksgiving, And into His courts with praise. Be thankful to Him, and bless His name. (Psalm 100:4 NKJV)

God inhabits the praises of His people. If I'm going to pray, I want to have that! I tried worshipping while sitting in my chair but it felt disrespectful at first. I chose to get on my knees and worship with my hands lifted in the air. The only problem with "waiting" like this, is that after a while (unless His spirit empowers you) my knees would get sore and my shoulders would get tires. I don't mind that sacrifice during worship but it shifted my attention from God to my sore knees and tired shoulders. I had to come up with a new plan.

I knew I wanted to be on my knees as an act of honor and respect so I decided to start my waiting in this way, but move to my prayer chair afterwards. Worship always varied depending on the leading of the Holy Spirit. It could be ten minutes or four hours. I tried to be led of the spirit throughout the whole process. On an average though, I would say that worship before waiting lasted about twenty minutes.

Coming into Rest

I would move to the prayer chair or sometimes lay on the floor but tried to keep that spirit of worship in my heart. One of the first things I would do in the chair was try to come to a place of rest. Why would I do this? Because the body, or the flesh wants to insert itself into everything including prayer time. I purposefully went through a mental check-list to determine if I was carrying stress or tension in my body.

I discovered this accidently it seemed one night as I was praying. I was trying too hard. I wanted a breakthrough so much I was bracing myself as if for impact. I realized that my jaw was set to the point where I began to feel discomfort. How do you wait and pray in that state? I had to calm down. I don't want my flesh to override the desires of my spirit. After a few times I started trying to notice from the top of my head to the bottom of my feet whether I was truly at rest. I learned that I had to do this many times at first, just to be able to discern the difference.

I made it an exercise to learn how to go from up and walking around to rest. Once I felt like I had done it, I would get up and walk around and then start again. What was the point in this? I didn't want every time to be a struggle. I wanted to learn to release this strife or struggle to the Lord and let it go so I could move straight to my prayer time.

Many times, people look at this practice and think "new age" or "meditation." Yes, I understand that. What is your focus and desire? Who are you looking at? When you hear someone threw a stick on the ground and it turned into a snake, are you thinking witchcraft or are you thinking Aaron? (Moses) To which camp do *you* belong? That makes all the difference in the world.

Being at rest is a huge thing in waiting on God. I can't overemphasize that.

When I'm Waiting, am I Doing Nothing?

No, no, no and no! Because we don't appear to be doing anything physical, some get the idea that we are doing nothing. I have heard a couple well-known ministers address this and they have made strong statements about waiting on the Lord in stillness being completely wrong and not helpful in bringing breakthrough in the things of the spirit. I don't like to contradict people but those ministers do not have an understanding of this.

If the Lord told you He was sending an angel to guard you and watch over you and then you saw the angel standing in your home at night, if the angel was standing still would you say he was doing nothing? Wow! You saw an angel? What was he doing? "Nothing." No, a correct answer would be he was standing guard over us to make sure we are protected and ok.

If the Lord shows up and you can't discern why or what He is doing, do you assume He is doing nothing? I sure hope not.

If you had a serious problem you needed to "think through" so you sat back and closed your eyes to think and concentrate, are you doing nothing? Herein lays much of the problem when we talk about the value and function of spiritual things. We live so much in the natural and in the flesh that doing something in the spirit, even for those who as believers should know it has value can't see it sometimes. A prayer has value and power and we don't even have to move or speak to release it.

I heard a "testimony" a few years ago where a minister was talking about visiting someone sick and dying in hospice care. He went to go show his concern and love for the person and as I listened, I thought it was such a kind and noble thing to do. Towards the end of his story he told the audience that he felt so helpless in the situation because he knew there was absolutely nothing that he could do to help the person. All he could do was be there and let them know that he cared. When he said those words, I thought here is a man that has come to believe that prayer has no power. A believer who faces any situation and yet believes there is no hope, is someone who has been misinformed horribly. Our God is merciful and powerful being our ability to comprehend it.

If you want to have any kind of understanding about the things of the spirit, you must understand that the things of the spirit don't always hinge themselves on the physical or works and action in the natural realm. Asa matter of fact even many believers think things of the spirit are foolishness.

But the natural man does not receive the things of the Spirit of God, for they are foolishness to him; nor can he know them, because they are spiritually discerned. (1Corinthians 2:14 NKJV)

What We do When We Wait

As I began to wait on the Lord, I chose to do it exactly as I had done it the first day because of the thing I had experienced. I would close my eyes and "look" with anticipation. What am I looking at?! That is a valid question and I hear it a lot!

I am not looking in an uninterested or disassociated way. Even though the color field before my closed eyes is usually black, almost black or light to dark grey, there are very, very subtle things going on in that "field" before me. Why the color variations? The light already present where you are will change what you initially see with your eyes closed. A good way to illustrate this is to close your eyes and turn your head towards a light. Now take your hand and wave it a few inches in front of your face. This is the effect I'm talking about.

I was doing more than looking though. I have explained it in the past as being as focused as a sentry on guard duty standing at attention and looking towards the dark and listening intently so that any movement or sound of any kind will be seen or heard. I noticed very soon that as I waited with this kind of expectation to see while my physical eyes were closed, actually caused my spiritual eyes to begin to open. When you look when there is nothing physical to see, a shift takes places and your spiritual eyes begin to engage.

I long for you more than any watchman would long for the morning light. I will watch and wait for you, O God, throughout the night. (Psalm 130:6 TPT)

So, I was doing much more than just sitting. I was examining the grey or dark field in front of my closed eyes and trying (from a place of rest) to notice any variation within it. I would see very, very faint lines or dots or movements of some kind. The longer I looked I would also see very faint colors come up and fade away and sometimes little barely noticeable flashes etc. What in the world does this have to do with the gospel?! You won't fully understand the implications until you can actually see and hear and navigate the spiritual realm the way we are supposed to. We are waiting on God not just to wait but to connect with the Lord in a deeper way, where we hear

His voice *clearly* and see what the Father is doing *clearly* just like the Lord talked about.

Then Jesus answered and said to them, "Most assuredly, I say to you, the Son can do nothing of Himself, but what He sees the Father do; for whatever He does, the Son also does in like manner. (John 5:19 NKJV)

Expectations of God

As I was waiting there was (and is) an expectation that He will show me or tell me or teach me something. Why would I believe that? I believe because if we ask for bread, He won't give us a stone. (Matthew 7:9) It is more than reasonable to expect God to answer the cry of our heart to know Him more.

This way of looking was my default position of waiting on the Lord. I all goes together however as I'm sure you understand. Starting with worship, move into stillness and close my eyes and look with expectation. I know it may sound like a lot of work but the whole thing is really quite simple and only requires that we spend time with Him in His presence. That isn't work right?

Some nights were very rewarding and other nights I felt that I had made no breakthrough. The thing that I had to remember was that I was coming before the Lord and there is no waste in that. In His presence is fullness of joy. We have to remember that.

Visitations of Angels

Because I am writing this with my journals laying open on my desk, I can see how the fruit of what I am telling you unfolded in my own life. For instance, twelve days after my initial experience my wife Gordana saw an angel in bodily form walk through our house. What I didn't realize at that time was that by my seeking the Lord this passionately it was causing Heaven to manifest in our home. This only increased and opened experiences with the Lord's angels appearing to our kids. That is the whole point to me. I have said it many times and I may well mention it again. I believe that we should come to a relationship with Christ that is so profound that all of Heaven opens to us.

I had many teaching moments from the Lord in this season that were relevant to me and my life and issues. You will have the same. Even the things I'm talking about, the Lord may very well give you an understanding tailor made for you. In fact, I know He will.

I remember one visitation I had while waiting on the Lord where an angel came and told me something very specific to this life I was seeking and the breakthrough I needed. The angel told me that my spiritual eyes had been damaged by all the garbage I had put into my eyes over the years. He also told me that the Lord could heal them. That was huge for my own journey. God has been giving me keys just like that and He will for you also.

Changing my Focus

Although I don't usually have any problems staying focused on looking with intention, occasionally I would be distracted by things I had seen during the day, things from TV or even situations that had stirred me up in the flesh. These random images would come to my mind and try to derail me from my purpose. I found that in those instances I had to give my mind something more to do.

Initially I would rebuke or cast down thoughts that were hindering by declaration either *in my mind or out loud with my mouth.*

"Thoughts not productive to what I'm doing I call you to cease from coming up before me." Or *"Ungodly thoughts I rebuke you and cast you down. You have no place in my thought life or mind."*

I found that changing my focus to something more active really helped with that. I would see in my imagination the Lord Jesus and I would bow before Him and worship Him. I would see Heaven in my imagination and the throne and I would make a mental image of things the bible talked about, spiritual scenes or passages that meant something to me. I found if I kept my mind occupied in these times it was easier to stay focused on the Lord. Did this change the result I was looking for? In doing this was I still making a connection with the Lord? Yes, very much so.

As we set this time aside to be with Him, He knows what we are doing and why. This is no surprise to Him and He is actually the one guiding us in this journey. We should know that. Just by waiting we honor Him. By imaging His face, we honor Him. By thinking about heavenly things, we honor Him. By worshipping even in our imaginations, we honor Him. Yes, all these things we do are valid and will yield fruit.

Those Who wait upon the Lord...

One of the most challenging issues I faced waiting on God was how to wait and not fall asleep. How do you work all day long, take care of household, kids and other responsibilities and pray and wait on God through the night? Sounds impossible. Early on after having written about spending a lot of time in prayer, I had many people contact me to find out the truth about this. What is the reality behind what you're saying? One pastor told me "I don't have time to pray like you are talking about it." Another man called and said "You people in ministry have nothing better to do anyway. Some of us have responsibilities!" Wow! At the time I was working a full-time job sixty hours a week, had family, home and various other things as well.

I don't want to discourage anyone. I'm not saying that God makes it almost impossible to spend time in His presence. He is doing a quick work and I have been beneficiary of prices that others have paid even in my own life. You have heard the saying "My ceiling can be your floor"? It is true. I have to be transparent about my own life though because I know that there are people who have looked for and believed for breakthrough in the things of the spirit for years and are frustrated as to why it hasn't come. I've been there and that why I share as openly as I do.

That being said, passion for God and for the things of God is not something you can do without. The pearl of great price parable is fitting concerning these things.

44 "Again, the kingdom of heaven is like treasure hidden in a field, which a man found and hid; and for joy over it he goes and sells all that he has and buys that field

45 "Again, the kingdom of heaven is like a merchant seeking beautiful pearls, 46 who, when he had found one pearl of great price, went and sold all that he had and bought it. (Matthew 13:44-46 NKJV)

I believe there has to be this kind of passion for the Lord and if you don't have it you should ask the Lord for it. Did King David wait on the Lord because he had nothing better to do? Of course not.

Still, I had an issue I was dealing with. I wanted to stay up and pray and wait on God but I was physically tired. I would go to my prayer chair at midnight, start to pray or wait and the next thing I knew it was morning and I was waking up. I spent ten minutes praying and the rest of the time sleeping. Sometimes I made it twenty minutes or a half hour. Many times I waited as long as an hour but in the end I would wake up realizing I had fallen asleep once again. It was a bit discouraging. The spirit was willing but the flesh was weak. Don't get me wrong. The Lord was still honoring my little steps of faith and when I look at my journal from that time period, I can see God's hand was all over it. This whole process, even with the mistakes and failures was all a part of my education in the things of the spirit.

Months had gone by and I was still sleeping through at least half of my prayer time. I would wake up in my chair at two, three or four in the morning and I would apologize to the Lord. "Lord, I'm sorry. I will try again tomorrow. One morning very early I woke up in the chair and I once again apologized and told the Lord I'll try again tomorrow, when I heard the Lord ask, "What's wrong with right now?" I sat there and continued to wait but fell asleep again and when I once again told the Lord I would try tomorrow He again said, "What's wrong with right now?" He did that three times.

The last time when I awoke, I awoke in the spirit. That is to say that my spiritual eyes and senses were wide open and I saw and experienced the spiritual realm with much more awareness than we experience the natural realm. I learned a very important lesson that night. Can you guess what it was? Don't quit. I also learned that at a certain point my physical body was not able to wake up but my spirit man did.

I learned much later that many saints of the past would tie themselves in an upright position so that they wouldn't fall asleep when they prayed. Although I never did that, I would get up if I felt tired and walk through the house praying until I felt awake again, and then resume waiting in my chair.

How did I solve the problem of little sleep? I really didn't. I continued on in relentless fashion because I *desired* that relationship with God that many talked about. Waking and continuing or getting up and walking/praying but eventually a grace came upon me to need very little sleep. I would pray and wait all night and catch an hour or two nap before having to go to work. I felt good. Many say that they couldn't continue on like this, that it would be hard to stay motivated. I haven't shared much about this part but I will tell you that one visitation from the Lord will compel you to spend your nights and days in waiting and in prayer. One visitation from an angel of the Lord will give you all the motivation you need to keep you running to your prayer closet at the end of the day.

In the end, ask the Lord for grace to pray and wait and remind Him of His promise. He will honor it.

But those who wait on the Lord Shall renew their strength; They shall mount up with wings like eagles, They shall run and not be weary, They shall walk and not faint. (Isaiah 40:31 NKJV)

Even though I was very much *learning* how to wait upon the Lord, this whole process was filled with breakthroughs, visitations and instruction. It was during this time that the Lord began to visit me in the night to teach me about spiritual sight and walking in the fullness of our spiritual senses. I can't tell you the number of times my spiritual eyes would suddenly open and I would see an angel close to me, looking into my eyes.

I had made a decision and God was meeting me. I was drawing close to Him and He was drawing close to me. Simple steps of Faith.

This was the beginning of my journey. It was all very simple but I can't say that it was completely easy. My flesh had to be trained to be quiet. When I began to wait in stillness, I constantly had to deal with my fleshes desire to move around. I had to make a choice every night... do I want to pray or am I too tired? On top of that, virtually no one in my world understood my desire to pray and wait on the Lord. Even the most "spiritual" people thought I was going overboard. Friends can carry a lot of weight to pull you back from the things of God. Your hunger makes people uncomfortable.

Be careful what you try to share.

Adjusting to the Spiritual Dimension

In the beginning of this book I shared a story of an encounter with an angel where, because of the power he carried, I literally ran out of the room. That was not an isolated incident. What happens when you wait on the Lord? The things of heaven begin to open around you. The more time you spend walking in the spirit, the more it becomes normal every-day life.

I was just re-reading some of my journal entries and saw that about a month after all this started the Lord Jesus appeared to my son Matt and prayed for him. Both he and my daughter Angie would see angels standing over them at night guarding them. Our home became a place of the manifest presence of God and the things of Heaven. There is no doubt that if you pursue the Lord His goodness will overtake you.

Before I share too much about the visitations that I believe were born out of living a life in pursuit of Him, I need to issue a caution. Because many if not most of us are at the beginning of learning about these things, it is critical that we follow biblical protocol in dealing with the manifestations of the spirit. In the book of first John chapter four.

Beloved, do not believe every spirit, but test the spirits, whether they are of God; because many false prophets have gone out into the world. 2 By this you know the Spirit of God: Every spirit that confesses that Jesus Christ has come in the flesh is of God, 3 and every spirit that does not confess [a]that Jesus [b]Christ has come in the flesh is not of God. And this is the spirit of the Antichrist, which you have heard was coming, and is now already in the world.

4 You are of God, little children, and have overcome them, because He who is in you is greater than he who is in the world. 5 They are of the world. Therefore, they speak as of the world, and the world hears them. 6 We are of God. He who knows God hears us; he who is not of God does not hear us. By this we know the spirit of truth and the spirit of error. (1 John 4:1-6 NKJV)

Waiting on the Lord gives you an open door to the things of the spirit so it's important to know that you have to test the spirits. If it were not a possibility that we were going to encounter this, the Lord would not have had John include it. Can I just say, don't come up with your own tests and don't forget to test the spirits EVERY TIME. I have had many encounters with evil spirits trying to pass themselves off as something they are not. Once during an encounter, I had a sense that this "angel" was not quite kosher, so to speak. When I pressed him he said "Everybody loves Jesus." Wrong answer. I've had people tell me they can discern by looking in their eyes and others have said they were embarrassed to ask. We are not playing games here.

I have often said that people say Christians should not "mess" with the supernatural. I say Christians should be the most supernatural people on the planet. But.... In agreement and in accordance with the word of God.

Heavenly Schools

One evening while in prayer I suddenly found myself in a place in Heaven where an angel was leading a class, teaching children of God to walk and move in "new shoes." I watched in amazement for a while and then got my new shoes as well, participating in the class.

Why did I share that? Because it doesn't feel "normal" to be praying in your house one minute and then look around to discover you are somewhere else. It is something you have to learn to expect.

The manifestation of the power angels carry can be very uncomfortable when you first begin to encounter it. Many times in the bible we see angels saying "Don't be afraid."

There is a good reason for that. During times of waiting on the Lord, sometimes you will feel the power or the glory they carry come upon you. It can feel like you are covered with a powerful electrical current. The truth is that if we feel this during corporate worship at church, it may seem somewhat normal but if you feel it at home by yourself in the middle of the night, you may need to remember the words "don't be afraid"

One day Gordana and I were praying in agreement for breakthrough in our upstairs bedroom when all of the sudden we heard what sounded like sleigh bells ringing in our walk-in closet. We don't have bells in our closet. I went in and looked around anyway and asked the Lord what it was. The Lord spoke to me and told me it was the bells on the bridles of the war horses. It had been in response to our prayer for breakthrough. Still not what most people would consider normal. I like to challenge people ... What kind of life do you really want?

Most of the time the angels around our lives are completely veiled so that we don't see them, feel them, hear them or sense their presence in any way. As you wait upon the Lord, that veil begins to fall. If we felt the full weight of the glory they carry we would probably fall down just like Daniel or John.

After a while in this life, I began to see a light at my left side ten to twenty times per day. I would see this especially during times of prayer and sometimes the light looked like a raging fire. In the beginning I thought I had something wrong with my eyes. It wasn't too long before I realized it was an angel that is with me a lot. His appearance is as fire but sometimes I can only see the light of the fire. Again, this is something that you will very probably see at some point as you wait on the Lord. He has made His angels to appear that way.

You make your messengers into winds of the Spirit and all your ministers become flames of fire. (Psalms 104:4 TPT)

Consider Daniel's encounter with Gabriel

4 Now on the twenty-fourth day of the first month, as I was by the side of the great river, that is, the [c]Tigris, 5 I lifted my eyes and looked, and behold, a certain man clothed in linen, whose waist was girded with gold of Uphaz! 6 His body was like beryl, his face like the appearance of lightning, his eyes like torches of fire, his arms and feet like burnished bronze in color, and the sound of his words like the voice of a multitude.

7 And I, Daniel, alone saw the vision, for the men who were with me did not see the vision; but a great terror fell upon them, so that they fled to hide themselves. 8 Therefore I was left alone when I saw this great vision, and no strength remained in me; for my [d]vigor was turned to [e]frailty in me, and I retained no strength. 9 Yet I heard the sound of his words; and while I heard the sound of his words I was in a deep sleep on my face, with my face to the ground.

10 Suddenly, a hand touched me, which made me tremble on my knees and on the palms of my hands. 11 And he said to me, "O Daniel, man greatly beloved, understand the words that I speak to you, and stand upright, for I have now been sent to you." While he was speaking this word to me, I stood trembling.

12 Then he said to me, "Do not fear, Daniel, for from the first day that you set your heart to understand, and to humble yourself before your God, your words were heard; and I have come because of your words. (Daniel 10:4-12 NKJV)

Am I saying that you could have encounters like Daniel? Yes, absolutely. I pray that you don't read about these encounters with God in the bible and think "oh how scary! I hope that never happens to me." I read those passages and say "Yes Lord! I want a life like that!"

Still, I have rebuked angels many times because I was not used to the manifestation of the things of the spirit in my life. A life focused on the natural will do that to you.

Chapter Four

Silence, Stillness and Rest

The Value of Silence

Silence is defined in the dictionary as

1. complete absence of sound.

synonyms: quietness, quiet, quietude, still, stillness, hush, tranquility, noiselessness, soundlessness, peace, peacefulness, peace and quiet.

Why do I value silence in waiting on the Lord? Natural sound is a connection to the natural realm. Sound in general (unless it is sound for a godly or spiritual purpose) can be a distraction in many ways. When we look at the Lord's revelation to Elijah, we can see the value of silence or quiet.

11 And he said, Go forth, and stand upon the mount before the Lord. And, behold, the Lord passed by, and a great and strong wind rent the mountains, and brake in pieces the rocks before the Lord; but the Lord was not in the wind: and after the wind an earthquake; but the Lord was not in the earthquake:

12 And after the earthquake a fire; but the Lord was not in the fire: and after the fire a still small voice.

13 And it was so, when Elijah heard it, that he wrapped his face in his mantle, and went out, and stood in the entering in of the cave. And, behold, there came a voice unto him, and said, What doest thou here, Elijah? (1 Kings 19:11-13 KJV)

The noise of the world will try to drown out not only the voice of God but the voice of your spirit and the voice of your

53

conscience. Silence is a place where you can hear your own thoughts and reflect on your life in God.

When you are waiting on the Lord you don't want anything in the way that might steal your attention or drown out what the Lord may be trying to reveal to you.

This analogy may be understood a bit more by those of us a few years older. If you are driving somewhere unfamiliar or during a rain storm at night, have you ever turned off the radio so that your focus is not diluted? Or if you think your car is making a strange noise you would turn off any competing noises so you can hear what is important. Lastly, have you ever tried to talk to someone about something important and they tell you "Go ahead. I can watch TV and still hear you just fine." I think most of us have experienced that.

When we come before the Lord in silence, we are making a statement. Lord there is nothing I want to hear more than your voice. What you have to say to me or show me is important. I'm not saying that we don't speak to God even in the hustle and bustle of our day but there is something special about hiding away with the Lord in silence to listen to His voice.

Here again, just as we learned about looking with eyes closed, when you listen when there are no natural sounds to hear, we begin to tune into the sounds of Heaven and the things of the spirit.

Hearing in the Spirit

Many times, in the absence of natural sound or noise, especially when waiting in anticipation, the sounds of Heaven can grow very loud. Hearing heavenly worship as you wait on the Lord will be a common thing to experience. Just enjoy it and lean into it.

Hearing Heaven at Work

After the Kingdom of Heaven began to manifest around my life, I would often hear heavenly worship at work. The first time it happened it really shocked me. I was standing at the parts sink not far from the tech's area when I began to hear the most beautiful music playing. I stood there at the sink really enjoying it when it hit me... I thought to myself, there is no one in this place that would be playing Christian music besides me.

After I got done at the sink, I went walking through the service area to see which tech had Christian music playing. Not one person had their radio playing yet the music was all around me. It was an incredible confirmation that the things of Heaven are available to us.

Once I knew that I could hear in the spirit even when in an environment not necessarily optimum for it, I began to listen for it and hear it much, much more.

The Value of Stillness

In a world filled with movement and action, activities and diversions it seems almost purposeful that the world doesn't want us to stop and think for a minute. We schedule our time many times so that we can keep moving and keep accomplishing our goals. If we are standing in a line, we want it to move faster. If we are hungry, many times we don't even take the time to sit and enjoy a meal. That would slow us down. Let's go through the drive-through and eat on the way. That way it only costs us eight minutes and we can keep moving.

We have a million things to keep us active and distracted. Music and television, i phones and i pads, our jobs and careers, hobbies, out to dinner, out with friends, church, Facebook, Twitter, Instagram and Snapchat. I know some people who don't have time for a prayer life because they can't fit it in between their Instagram posts! I'm only partly kidding about that. We are literally trained to stay busy and we are used to it and we are very good at it. What we are not so good at is being still or quiet.

Stillness and the value of stillness just isn't something we were raised with. Most of us have never been taught the principle or value of stillness anywhere, especially not at church.

Be still, and know that I am God; I will be exalted among the nations, I will be exalted in the earth! (Psalms 46:10 NKJV)

So, what is the deal about being still? Isn't this overkill? Can't God hear us when we pray on the move? Can't we feel His presence even if we are busy? Can't I be a good and productive Christian and not worry about this stillness? Can I be a lover of Jesus, dedicated to Him and living for Him and not do all this stuff?

Once again we come to "What kind of life do you want?"

When I talk at the Schools of the Supernatural for Bruce Allen's ministry, I share about stillness to the point where it makes people uncomfortable. Get yourself ready to be uncomfortable. I'm not trying to be contentious I just feel that we don't have time to play games or beat around the bush. People need to know how to get a breakthrough into the supernatural things of God now, not twenty years from now! Souls are hanging in the balance and brothers and sisters are crying out for deliverance and healing. Will you be the one to step up even if it makes you a bit uncomfortable? Right now, I'm seeing a vision of Isaiah lifting his hand high and saying "Here am I lord. Send me!" (Isaiah 6:8) I believe there are many willing to step up and walk in God's power for such a time as this.

Why do people get uncomfortable? Because most are not used to be taken through an exercise to come to a place of rest. It seems "new age" to most.

Coming to Stillness/Rest Overview

Get into the place where you are going to be praying, whether that be your prayer closet, prayer chair, bed, office or wherever you feel led by the spirit to pray. Now, close your eyes and take a couple deep breaths.

We are going to learn how to take our flesh out of the equation as we pray. We don't want the flesh to be a distraction so we are doing something to give the flesh a little "time out."

Just sit still for a minute. Now, starting at the top of your head, go through a check-list in your mind questioning yourself if each part of your body is at rest. When I did this, I would ask myself, "Is my head at rest? Is my face at rest? I know, it sounds kind of funny but the truth is, and I mentioned it earlier, that we tense up sometimes when we pray and it becomes a distraction. I go through the whole list slowly... neck, shoulders, arms, forearms, hands, chest, back, stomach, hips, legs, knees, calves, ankles and feet.

Many, many times I ask myself "Is this at rest?" and the answer is no, so I try to purposely bring that area of my body to rest and then continue. I will go through this exercise many times. I don't want my flesh to be a stumbling block in any way.

What is the spiritual implication of this? You are crucifying your flesh. Your flesh normally will not like this. We are not used to it. We are so not used to it we don't even stay still when we sleep.

What is the practical implication? We are striving to come into His rest.

9 There remaineth therefore a rest to the people of God. 10 For he that is entered into his rest, he also hath ceased from his own works, as God did from his. 11 Let us labour therefore to enter into that rest, lest any man fall after the same example of unbelief. (Hebrews 4:9-11 KJV)

When you are in stillness waiting on the Lord, you begin to have an awareness of your spirit that you may have never had before. We have been so consumed with the physical, it's all we know for the most part. Once the flesh has no say, the spirit man is in first place or leadership role. How is that? Because your flesh is quite and you are only focused on the Lord, worshipping the Lord and praying to the Lord.

Why do we have to practice this? Because we already know how to be physical. We know how to walk, eat, run, talk, yell, jump, move etc., we just need to know how to be still. I understand that we need to be instant in season and out of season. It's not like we can run to the prayer closet every time someone needs prayer or we need to hear from God. That isn't what we are doing here. We are learning a practical application to use in our pursuit of waiting on the Lord.

Once we get the breakthrough, the dynamic changes. It's kind of like if you were being taught to juggle and ride a unicycle. You theoretically could learn to do both at the same time. However, when people learn these skills, they learn them separately and master them separately before joining them together. It is practical. What about biblical?

Well, there is no scripture that I am aware of that tells you to come to rest one body part at a time. I'll grant you that. Just because something isn't mentioned in the bible doesn't mean it is unbiblical. We should understand this. For instance, if I told you that when you memorize scriptures it helps to read them through three or four times and you should not be watching TV when you do it. You could respond by telling me that the word TV isn't mentioned anywhere in the bible, but of course we know I'm just giving a practical suggestion to help further our knowledge of God.

In the same way, we learn to make our flesh quiet so our spirit man comes to the forefront and leads the way for a change. As we do this, we get breakthrough into the things of the spirit. It's in this place that we begin to encounter God as we never have before.

Expectation

Expectation is a strong belief that something is going to happen. Expectation is in itself a step of faith or a proof of faith. We believe God therefor we expect Him to honor His word.

God is not a man, that He should lie, Nor a son of man, that He should repent. Has He said, and will He not do? Or has He spoken, and will He not make it good? (Numbers 23:19 NKJV)

Expectation (or faith) is what leads us to pray and worship, expectation leads us to pray for the sick believing God to heal them.

But without faith it is impossible to please Him, for he who comes to God must believe that He is, and that He is a rewarder of those who diligently seek Him. (Hebrews 11:6 NKJV)

This expectation is what causes me to go to my prayer chair every night and wait and look for what God wants to show me. I had this expectation because I heard someone's testimony. After hearing I tried it for myself. I had an expectation but since God has proven His faithfulness in this, my expectation is even much greater. I realize that if God does not honor His word, if we can't trust Him, then what are we even doing? I believe. We have taught this principle of waiting on God to people all over the world and we see breakthrough after breakthrough of the things of the kingdom being open to them.

Many have the idea that they have to "feel" some great level of expectation or faith. "I'd like to believe but I don't feel I have that kind of faith." So, how much faith do we have to have? How much expectation do we have to have? We just have to have enough to take the step of faith. We only need to follow the instruction to wait upon the Lord. This step of faith is the faith we need. Seems too simple.

Down deep you know what you really believe. Doubt and self-doubt, skepticism and unbelief try to influence our thoughts and minds, creating the idea that we don't *really* believe or we don't *really* have that much faith. The truth is that if you didn't believe, you would not pray. If you didn't expect, you wouldn't be up in the middle of the night waiting on the Lord. You actually do believe and you do expect. Don't let the enemy talk you out of it.

Raising the Level

We can raise the level of our expectation. We can believe for more and receive it. How do we do this? One of the easiest ways is to dig out testimonies on YouTube or some other medium and feed on them every day. Personally, I would line up a dozen or so testimonies on separate pages on my computer and watch them one right after the other. It is hard *not* to take that boost of faith with you into prayer.

Another thing you can do is join groups where people are seeking the deeper things of God. You can know who they are by the fact that Jesus is about the only thing they like to talk about. If you don't have groups like this in your church or area, there are many springing up all over online on Facebook or other places. Another thing to keep your expectation high is to not share what God is doing in your life with those who have no value for it. Trying to share with people like that can discourage you at best and cause you to give up or also not believe at worst.

I know that is a difficult thing to do. We have friends that have problems and we think "If they could only feel God's presence the way I do it could change everything for them." Many will have to be shown by the Holy Spirit. They, sorry to say, don't want to believe. I went to speak at a church once and had the honor of staying at the pastor's home. As I shared the things I believed and experienced at his dining room table, he let me know that those things were not important and a true man of God wouldn't care about walking in the miraculous. I didn't push it but his buttons had definitely been pushed. Before I left the following day, his contempt had risen to the level where he was actually mocking me openly. It is hard to pursue the things of God with joy in that kind of atmosphere. Share with those who honor God, who honor what God is doing and who honor you as a friend.

Chapter Five

Practical Steps

In my own life I have boiled down the things I do into practical steps that I do every day. I'm not talking about doing things by rote or coming up with a system to "activate" God. We don't have to "activate" God as He is the one calling and drawing us, wooing us by His Spirit. Rest assured that He is not the problem. No, I'm talking about giving the things of the spirit at least the same weight we give to the rest of our lives. Having lists and plans so that we don't forget to do things that are important. It's kind of like, I will start my day in prayer and study and meditate on the word before I go to sleep. Practical things we can do to have a closer walk with the Lord.

Waiting on God in the Morning

On days that I don't immediately have to get out of bed and get going, When I awake, usually somewhere between six and seven, I will lay in bed and wait on the Lord. I don't move around too much as I don't want to be too physical. Even though I have just woken up, I will lay on my back (sometimes my side) and come into rest the way I have described it earlier. I close my eyes and look at (for) the spiritual dimension with my eyes closed. Sometimes during this morning period I find myself actually drifting back to sleep, but having incredibly realistic dreams and visions where the Lord speaks. It's a great way to start the day.

Waiting in the car

Don't think I've gone overboard yet. If I have to drive somewhere, when I arrive I take five minutes and still myself and wait on the Lord. I "look" for His presence upon me. I try to sense or feel His fire or light clothing me. I imagine this sometimes to start and this step of faith will often allow me to feel the reality of it. I want to be aware of His presence so that I take that with me wherever I go. I wan to take the conscious knowledge that He is with me.

Waiting at Work

If you haven't already figured it out, I don't wait for night to practice waiting on the Lord. I try to make this my default position day and night. I engage as often as I can and at work that is usually at least three times per day. We have lunch break, and two other breaks in the morning and afternoon. Usually I have taken lunch at odd times so that I can have the breakroom to myself and wait on the Lord at one of the lunch tables. Other times I would sit on the bench in the washroom.

Practicing waiting on the Lord at work has been nearly as fruitful as waiting at home. Because I am staying conscious of the spiritual realm while at work, I have seen angels openly many times but I have seen demons as well. There was a co-worker who saw what he claimed was a giant being the size of a large bear in the machine storage area. I sensed something there but did not see it. He was terrified and would not go into that area. About two years later I saw it. I was about ten feet tall and big like a bear or gorilla. Of course, it was an evil spirit and no worries because we have authority over them. I noticed him because as I was walking through the storage area, he was pacing me about two rows over. I rebuked him and told him he couldn't stay. He had to go and he did.

Waiting in the Watch of the Night

Probably my favorite time for prayer and waiting on God. Starting time varies now but often carries on until morning. I begin waiting just as I have described. There are variations depending on what I feel the Holy Spirit is telling me. (We should be led of the spirit through all of this) Looking and examining the atmosphere before me, looking for small and almost imperceptible movements has been a place of breakthrough for me.

Also, visiting Heaven in my imagination as I wait has also been a place of breakthrough.

1 Christ's resurrection is your resurrection too. This is why we are to yearn for all that is above, for that's where Christ sits enthroned at the place of all power, honor, and authority![a] 2 Yes, feast on all the treasures of the heavenly realm and fill your thoughts with heavenly realities, and not with the distractions of the natural realm.

3 Your crucifixion[b] with Christ has severed the tie to this life, and now your true life is hidden away in God in Christ. 4 And as Christ himself is seen for who he really is, who you really are will also be revealed, for you are now one with him in his glory! (Colossians 3:1-4 TPT)

The Lord had taken me to a place in Heaven once where there was a wonderful park with beautiful paths and a large hall with paintings lining the hallway. I went back there in my imagination, remembering the details of the place as well as I could. We are called to think on such things.

I want to mention two other things that are important although I don't want you to get sidetracked. The thing is that many, many people get the idea that the more they learn about something, the easier it becomes to walk in those things. I have not found that to be so neither from my own life nor from the lives of those who believed it would be so. We were doing a school once and there were people there who told me they were very advanced in the things of the spirit. I said "great!" They knew names of angels and archangels, they knew protocols of Heaven, they knew which angel held which key to which door and a bunch of other stuff.

After spending some time with them, talking and listening to the questions they asked, I realized they were not actually walking in the things they knew so much about. Greater knowledge doesn't always get you the breakthrough. I say this because when the Lord Jesus taught me about spiritual sight and the things of the spirit, He made everything very simple for me. Nothing He shared with me was difficult to understand or to do. In many things in life it seems, if you master one small thing, it gives entrance to something bigger. This is why I so firmly believe waiting on the Lord will give you entrance into the things of Heaven. It is very simple, but if you master this it is yours.

Having said that, let me tell you about...

Waiting in Worship

Yet You are holy, O You who [a]are enthroned upon the praises of Israel. (Psalms 22:3 NASB)

Yet I know that you are most holy; it's indisputable. You are God-Enthroned, surrounded with songs, living among the shouts of praise of your princely people. (Psalms 22:3 TPT)

I remember several years ago I had gone to my prayer chair and decided I would worship for a little while and then wait and pray. I got lost in the presence of the Lord and time never seemed to pass. I found myself in the morning still sitting with my hands raised to Heaven worshipping. It was an incredible night and I didn't remember a time I had felt so alive. I had realized it was morning because I noticed light coming through the windows and remember thinking that I'd better go to bed and get an hour sleep before work.

I got up from the chair and walked around through our house. I had a drink of water and went to go outside to get a breath of the cool morning air when suddenly I found myself in another place. The Lord had translated me just like he had done to Philip. Please don't try to convince me it didn't happen or God doesn't do that. I was wide awake and walking when it happened.... Right after a night of worship.

Another time I got swept up in worshipping the Lord and suddenly I saw that the room was filled with angels. All different sizes and many were dressed differently. Yet another time during worship the fire of God fell upon me for a long time.

Setting yourself aside for God causes the things of Heaven to be manifest in your life.

Waiting in prayer and Intercession

During this time of learning I had several burdens on my heart to pray over. Many times, I would take these burdens to my prayer chair. Why did I do this? I was getting breakthrough in the realm of the spirit as I waiting on the Lord and believed that this breakthrough would also manifest on behalf of the situations that I was praying for. I was not disappointed.

I would usually always start in the same way with worship but then begin to silently lift up the needs of those I was praying for. Sometimes I would intercede for several hours and only have the knowing that God's word does not return void. His word is powerful whether we feel something happened or not. Other times the spiritual realm would open before me and I would see situations and answers to the things I was praying about. I remember once praying for a co-worker and asking the Lord what it was that was keeping him from yielding to the Lord. A vision opened before me and I saw into his house and I saw very clearly the battle he was facing. In that moment the Lord had shown me what to pray for.

Another time as I sought to do warfare and intercession an angel appeared before me and corrected me in what I was doing. He gave me a strategy of Heaven to help me to pray with authority and in God's perfect will.

During times of intercession for my children, because I was quiet and still before God I heard with such clarity, I knew what my kids were doing, who they were with, where they were going, addresses of houses I had never been to and phone numbers where they could be reached. Don't you believe that God wants us to operate in the fulness of Him for His glory and so that we can be effective for His kingdom? If we can just use the time we do have to come before Him our lives would never be the same.

Personally, I don't have a problem with spending so much time in His presence. I know we have things to do and I'm not talking about not fulfilling our obligations. I once met a dear woman of God who told me the Lord told her to lock herself away for two months and pray. She notified everyone she knew that she would not be available, unplugged her phone and spent the next two months alone with the Lord. She told me that when she came out of that house, she literally knew everything about everybody. She said her words of knowledge were so flowing and so accurate that it scared her. Many people came to Christ because of that. Ask yourself the question... is it worth two months of my life to walk in the gifts of God so powerfully. What if she would have told the Lord she didn't want to or didn't have time? Do we consider the things of God a pearl of great price?

Chapter Six

Overcoming Distractions

We deal with distractions every day. There are always people, things and situations that cry out for our attention and they want it right now. The thing is that we have to learn to deal with these things so that they don't derail our walk with God or our prayer life. Dealing with the kinds of distractions that are concerning our prayer lives, we have physical, mental/emotional and spiritual distractions that can affect us.

There are things we can do to silence the distractions.

Decide Beforehand

Make a decision about how you are going to deal with things that come up before you actually encounter them. The phone rings? The phone chirps (someone's messaged you) Someone interrupts you "I'm sorry, I know you said don't interrupt but this will only take a second..."

Decide going in how you are going to deal with things like this.

Anything physical that could derail you, take it out of the equation. When I used to kneel at my bedside to pray, there was a digital clock that I could see clearly from my vantage point. Sometimes when I would pray, I would start thinking and wondering how much time had passed. Invariably I would open my eyes and look at the clock. Move the clock or move to a different place.

Take off your glasses, make sure your clothes are comfortable enough not to be a distraction, turn your phone off, don't leave the TV on for light. It amazes me how the phone has become a common nuisance at church. At work we were forbidden from being on our phones during working hours except for emergency. At church you can see half the people on their phones at any given time during a message. You want to give them the benefit of the doubt and believe they are using the phone as a bible, but when your phone vibrates in your pocket you discover later that they were posting pictures to Facebook it makes you wonder...

We should be singular of purpose when we are waiting on God in prayer.

Some of the other physical distractions are the matters of home life that I talked about earlier. In matters of grave importance, I believe we can ask for solitude to pray for a season. In our normal prayer life however I don't think we can expect that. If you are a husband, father or son, those titles carry responsibilities and if you are a wife, mother or daughter you also have responsibilities as well. I learned that I could not expect my wife and kids to stay quiet in the house during the daytime. It just isn't a reasonable expectation.

However, I believe it is reasonable that during the night when one normally sleeps, it is not unreasonable to expect people to sleep as usual and allow me my time with God uninterrupted.

For those of you who have babies, we know that babies don't understand these rules. That is when it becomes more important to seek God and wait on the Lord in free moments during the day which I spoke of earlier. When we have seemingly limited time to spend in this pursuit due to no fault of our own, it becomes important to learn to stay connected to the Lord much like Brother Lawrence talks about in his book "Practicing the Presence of God".

Thoughts and Feelings

You will keep him in perfect peace, Whose mind is stayed on You, Because he trusts in You. (Isaiah 26:3 NKJV)

It can be hard to pray or wait when our thoughts keep running on in different directions. We do have things that happen during the course of a day but it should not overpower us or our minds and souls. To keep our souls at rest and at peace we have to be grounded with a firm foundation. In general, if you have problems keeping your thoughts from running away with you, spend more time in the word. Fill your soul with the power of His word. Meditate with your mind on His word. Realize that we are in Him. Apart from Him we can do nothing.

I am the vine, you are the branches. He who abides in Me, and I in him, bears much fruit; for without Me you can do nothing. (John 15:5 NKJV)

If you abide in Me, and My words abide in you, you[b] will ask what you desire, and it shall be done for you. 8 By this My Father is glorified, that you bear much fruit; so you will be My disciples. (John 15:7 NKJV)

Something that we have to realize also is that sometimes it takes a little time to retrain ourselves to think properly. We have spent a lifetime building an untrained and undisciplined mind and it may take some time to see things brought back to godly order. The good news is that your passion can speed up the process.

This time of quiet can sometimes be a catalyst for worries and fears to come up. When we are occupied and busy, we can redirect those kinds of thoughts but when we are still and quiet, we may have to deal with them more direct. For worries of the soul reading the Psalms is wonderful for bringing peace. Another thing to remember is that when our thoughts don't follow our directions, we have authority in Christ to deal with it.

Casting down imaginations, and every high thing that exalteth itself against the knowledge of God, and bringing into captivity every thought to the obedience of Christ; (2 Corinthians 10:5 NKJV)

Sometimes our souls/minds just need to be soothed and comforted. Some of the soaking music that is available today is really a blessing and anointed to do just that. We remember in first Samuel David's music refreshed Saul.

And it came to pass, when the evil spirit from God was upon Saul, that David took an harp, and played with his hand: so Saul was refreshed, and was well, and the evil spirit departed from him. (1 Samuel 16:23 KJV)

Take advantage of calm and quiet soaking music and if you have to use it all the time, do it. The Lord will lead you and give grace for your own journey just like He has done with mine.

Spiritual Distractions

When you are trying to get close to the Lord, hear His voice, see what the Father is doing and fulfill your purpose in God, you will very probably face opposition from the enemy. He doesn't want you to be effective in the kingdom. He doesn't want you to see or hear or feel or know. He will encourage you to be religious but he surely does not want you operating in the power of God.

This is something the Lord has had to remind me of several times so I know it is important.

Knowing that the enemy does not want people walking in power, I would spend the first hour of every day covering my family, home, work, finances, relations etc., with the blood of Jesus. Having had to deal with evil spirits sometimes I knew I needed to be diligent for the sake of my family. Over the course of a few years, things were going well and I was distracted with work and I let my guard down a bit. One day I had a dream that turned into a vision that turned into an encounter with an angel to remind me to do the things I was told to do.

Dream, Vision and Visitation

One night I dreamed that I was awoken by loud noises downstairs in our house. I went downstairs to investigate and found a rebellious group of kids smoking and drinking and breaking things and stealing things. I was so upset. In the middle of the room a man sat, watching everything go on. I couldn't get the troublemakers to stop and at this point as I inserted myself into trying to deal with it, it opened into an interactive vision. I was aware that I had to do something because the safety of my family depended on it.

Since I had no success earlier getting them to stop, I took my family out and was trying to leave for a safer place. As I started to leave, the man who had been sitting and watching stood in front of me preventing me from leaving. I was very angry and I said "That's it!" I walked up to him and as I got close to him, I realized he was an angel and at that moment he manifested his presence to me. As I stood there in front of this angel, I had instant knowledge that the power and authority he carried was for my benefit and I didn't need to be the one leaving. I needed to kick the trouble makers out and become diligent again to pray. As soon as this revelation was given to me, the angel reached out and lightly smacked me on top of the head, bringing back to the natural realm.

That was just one visitation of many where the Lord has reminded me to be aware and be a good watchman.

This is why when I wait upon the Lord, I first cover myself, my prayer time, my home (or wherever I'm praying) with the blood of Jesus. I ask for angelic help to surround and protect and to help see the will of God manifested in my life. I bind the work of the enemy and I bind all hindering spirits and spirits of lying and deception from operating, in Jesus' name.

Distractions or not I would suggest that you do the same.

Chapter Seven

Most Asked Questions

This chapter of questions will be active to receive new questions on this topic. Many people have questions that are specific to them that I may not have considered and I want to be available to answer them if I am able.

Those who may have questions can either present them in the book review section or send them to me via my website www.michaelvanvlymen.com or through messenger on Facebook. I will add the question to the chapter along with the answer.

Question: Does it always take so many hours in prayer to get breakthrough into the supernatural things of God?

Answer: The short answer is no, it does not. I outlined my personal journey in which dealing with things of my past took a little time. The important thing, the thing you can't be without is passion for God. If your attitude is that these things would be nice but you are fine if it never happens for you, chances are you will not experience these things. My wife spends little time set aside for prayer but prays all through the day. Her passion for God is challenging to most. One thing about her... many times the holy Spirit will lead her to intercede and she will spend as much as four or five hours in intercession. As the Spirit lads though, it isn't a time she has come up with. The things of Heaven are open to her.

Question: How do you spend hours waiting on God?

Answer: I do spend hours sometimes but it has been a process for me. Many people wonder how can you pray that long and what would you even say? The truth is that if I am praying in that way most of the time I am praying in tongues. You can literally pray in tongues for hours and not get tired or bored or feel like you are repeating yourself. Other times, my waiting turns into an encounter with the Lord. So, although I am sitting in my chair in the natural, in the spirit I am listening or learning or just paying attention to what God is doing. Also, when you wait on God in worship you can often get swept away in His presence and lose track of time. The thing is don't feel condemned about the time issue. The important thing is to ask the Lord what your journey is supposed to look like and do that. That is where your breakthrough will be. Always enjoy the time you spend with Him.

Question: How do you still your mind when you are waiting on God?

Answer: In your original question you stated that worship helps you to do that. Yes, I concur. The way we still our mind is not emptying it like some people think but rather keeping our minds stayed or fixed on Him. Worship is indeed an excellent way to do that. Another way is meditating or thinking about a facet of God...His beauty, His love, His grace, His sacrifice etc.. We give our minds something godly to do. In my own case my mind is very active in looking and examining the spiritual atmosphere before me.

Question: How do you deal with an overactive mind when waiting on God?

Answer: If you are an overly sensitive person perhaps you are always thinking about things going on in life. In the world they would tell a person to meditate in some new age way. The bible says You will keep him in perfect peace, Whose mind is stayed on You, Because he trusts in You. (Isaiah 26:3 NKJV)

Yes, according to the word, fix your mind on something...His word. Meditate on the word, especially the Psalms. We also have to remember that we have a loving Father who wants us to have the peace we need to pray and wait upon Him. Ask Him for that grace until it shows up. In my own life I had a season where these crazy and seemingly random thought would come when I was trying to pray and wait on the Lord. I finally got up from my chair one day and just began covering or applying the blood of Jesus over my thoughts, my mind, my dreams, my imagination, my memories and even the framework by which I reasoned and thought. I did this for about forty-five minutes and later when I went back to pray, I didn't have to deal with it. It took several times for me doing this but eventually I couldn't even make myself remember the stuff that had been bothering me. Do that as well.

Question: How do you wait on God when you have young kids or a family who doesn't appreciate you spending so much time doing this?

Answer: Having young kids or other responsibilities is definitely something that affects our choices in this. I understand also that when you talk about young children, usually the mother is the one who has to invest her time in the kids more. When I first had this challenge my kids were five and seven years old, not that I was waiting on God because I didn't know about that, but I would get up at four am to watch Dr. Lester Sumrall to learn, I was involved in deliverance ministry then and would often intercede and pray through the night for people. I also had time restrictions in that I was working sixty hours a week and also had responsibilities doing things with the family and taking care of the house. My evenings were not my own. Many times, I would go to bed and then I would get up from bed an hour later and go to pray. I'm not saying it was or is easy. It is simple, but not easy. What I have come to know is passion for the Lord is paramount and if you have little or no time, you must practice His presence so that you are always making the connection with the Lord. It is hard to pray in the night and work all day. I was blessed in that I had a job where I didn't have to think too much or deal with the public so that made it a bit easier.

Question: How do you deal with a roommate who works the same shifts as you? (I'm assuming this means you have little time alone)

Answer: Once again, circumstances beyond our control playing havoc with our prayer life. We want to pray and wait in stillness but we can't get a break sometimes. Again, I will say learn to practice the presence of God as you go through the day. This was something the Lord really impressed upon me as I was learning to walk in or be aware of both realms at the same time. Always thinking about the Lord and "seeing: Him next to you throughout your day will give you the breakthrough you desire.

Question: What makes the stillness that a Christian practices different from the stillness those in the new age practice?

Answer: Stillness is really a tool. Anyone can be still for any reason they choose. What makes it different for us is that we do what we do by the leading of the Holy Spirit to be and do what He wants us to be and do. Our focus is the Lord, our heart is for Him and we are doing this for an entirely different reason. It's kind of like learning to drive a car... anyone can do it, saved or unsaved, but where are you driving to? Are you going to do the work of the Lord, going to church or feeding the homeless or are you driving to the bar to drink and carouse and cause trouble? Any similarity is because the world has laid claim to many things that belong to the church and most of the church doesn't even realize it.

Question: How do you know when to engage and how to engage so as to honor the Glory and let God do what He's doing without missing it?

Answer: As with anything we are doing, we must be led of the spirit. Sometimes in my own life I pray and sometimes I intercede. Sometimes I worship and other times I just rest in His presence. I always try to be led of the spirit. I have had many times where I went to the chair to wait and heard the Lord say pray for so and so. The only way we can honor what He is doing is to hear His voice and obey it I believe.

Question: How do you self-evaluate with regard to the difference between waiting - and avoiding or putting on hold, or denying, or resignation?

Answer: The way we are waiting is with an expectation that He will speak to us or show us His will or His answer. That I think is the difference. If we wait without expectation then we might get caught in that trap but as long as we expect God to answer I think we are ok.

Question: Do you go through any 'activation' prior to being still. Eg - saying "I welcome you Jesus/Holy Spirit to show me anything you want me to see" or anything similar?

Answer: Another great question. It seems that when I pray in my chair, I already have an expectation that Jesus will come and show me what He wants to show me even though I don't actually say it. But, when I wait on my bed or on the floor, for some reason I do ask. "Lord please teach me something or show me something."

Question: Is there a prime time, spiritually speaking, for waiting on the Lord?

Answer: Many people I respect have told me that the third and fourth watch of the night is a time where the things of the spirit seem to be more accessible. (midnight – 3am / 3am – 6am) I also favor 3am as I have woken up to that exact time many, many times and have had many encounters with the things of Heaven at 3am.

Question: You have mentioned in previous posts when interceding and praying for hours this is accomplished by a lot of praying in the spirit. In intercession, is this followed by long periods of waiting expectantly in complete stillness & silence?

Answer: In general, I usually don't tie them together. The notable exception would be when I am interceding and asking for an answer or a direction or strategy, I would them wait and expect to hear something, so in that case yes, definitely. Other times I have interceded for a portion of the night and then waited upon the Lord.

Question: In spending hours waiting on God, is praying in tongues interspersed in there? I seem to remember reading that you walked around and prayed in the spirit to stay awake late at night/early mornings while waiting on God.

Answer: Yes. Many times, it is hard to stay awake while waiting in stillness. Many times, I have gotten up to walk through the house praying in tongues for anywhere from ten minutes to a couple of hours, depending on my physical state and the leading of the spirit.

Question: it's REALLY hard to maintain expectation in silence after 45 mins. to an hour of not seeing/hearing anything.

Answer: Ok, technically that was not a question, but I'll try to speak to it anyway. If you wait on God for forty-five minutes and see and hear nothing your level of expectation and excitement will be different than it would if you waited and suddenly an angel showed up and gave you a message. One time of waiting you would probably be thrilled over and the other not so much. The great thing is that your breakthrough to seeing and hearing isn't hinging on your level of excitement in your expectation. The level of expectation we need to see breakthrough is enough expectation to wait. We also can't forget... we are not waiting randomly but we are waiting in the presence of God and honoring Him by believing Him. It is much more compelling to wait once you begin to see and hear.

A FINAL WORD

I pray that you are encourage to wait on God after reading this little book. If anything, do NOT be discouraged. It is the Father's good pleasure to give you the kingdom. These desires you have to experience His presence and His glory, the desires you have to lay hold of all the things that the bible talks about and the saints of old walked in was placed in you by the Lord. He is the one who gives us passion for Him and to live for Him.

In the beginning of this book I shared an encounter I had where the Lord kept asking me if I wanted to stay and see what He had for me or if I wanted to run away. I believe that is the question the Lord is asking all of us in this hour. When you wait on the Lord there will almost certainly be a learning curve. You may not quite know what you're doing. It may feel tedious at times. It may be difficult. It may be challenging. You will experience things that most of the modern church has no grid for. It will certainly draw you closer to His side and cause you to know Him and to love Him like you never have before. The only question... Will you stay and see what He has for you?

ABOUT THE AUTHOR

MICHAEL VAN VLYMEN

Michael Van Vlymen is an author and speaker who teaches about the supernatural things of God. It's Michael's passion to share that everyone can learn to see in the spirit realm and walk in the supernatural.

Michael's Books

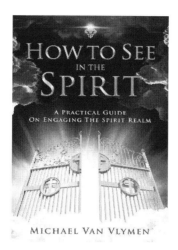

https://amzn.to/2YcmBiT

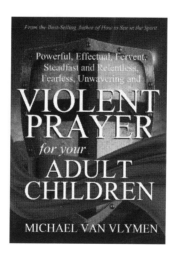

https://amzn.to/2XTHUGB

https://amzn.to/2XY4he0

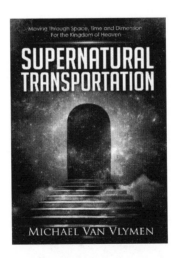

https://amzn.to/2Sw8zn5

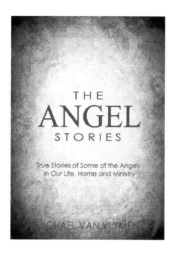

https://amzn.to/2Yo3LHD

Read these books and more at Amazon

Printed in Great Britain
by Amazon